TOURING GUIDE TO WILTSHIRE VILLAGES

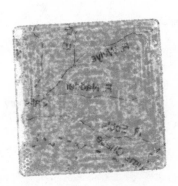

Cover: Castle Combe
(photograph courtesy of Jim Lowe, A.R.P.S., A.B.I.P.P.)

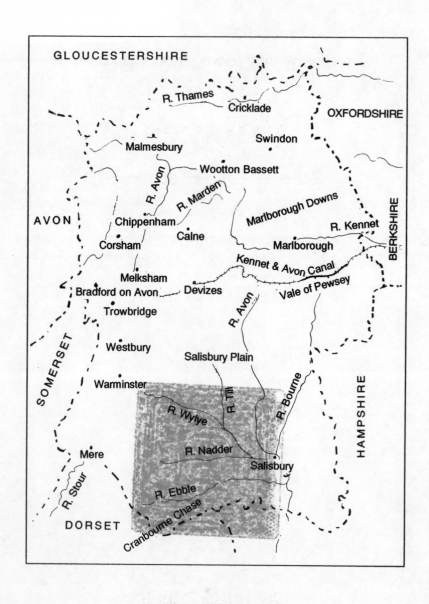

Touring Guide to
Wiltshire Villages

Margaret Wilson

Illustrated by Juliet Greaves

EX LIBRIS PRESS

First published 1987
This new edition published 1991 by

EX LIBRIS PRESS
1 The Shambles
Bradford on Avon
Wiltshire

Typeset in 10 point Palatino
Design and origination by Ex Libris Press

Printed by BPCC Wheatons Ltd., Exeter

ISBN 0 948578 29 7

To Michael — for help, interest and encouragement

We do not connect the same feelings with the works of art as with those of Nature, because we refer them to man, and associate with them the separate interests and passions which we know belong to those who are the objects, as a cottage, or a village church, which excites in us the same sensations as the sight of Nature, and which are, indeed, almost always included in descriptions of natural scenery.

Which is in part, no doubt, because they are surrounded with natural objects, and, in populous country, inseparable from them; and also because the human interest they excite relates to manners and feelings which are simple, common, such as all can enter into, and which, therefore, almost always produce a pleasing effect upon the mind.

Wiilliam Hazlitt, *On the Love of the Country,* **1814**

CONTENTS

6

Introduction

This is a book about the large and small villages of Wiltshire. Some of them are within hailing distance of the larger towns, some are remote and almost forgotten. All reach back down the centuries and provide a rich, human way of life which comes alive in the writings of John Aubrey, Richard Jefferies, Alfred Williams, and, more recently, Ida Gandy, Ralph Whitlock, A.G.Street, Pamela Street, Robin and Heather Tanner and others, most of whom were born in Wiltshire and loved to describe its way of life. The villages are the backbone of the county; no two are alike and the villages in the north of Wiltshire, due largely to its geological structure, are very different from those in the south.

Wiltshire's geological make-up provides the county with its most appealing feature — its downland landscape. Prehistoric man lived on these undulating chalk hills, and provided Europe with some of its richest monuments; Avebury and much of Stonehenge were created from the grey sandstone boulders known as sarsen stones (or 'grey wethers') which lie scattered over the chalk in the east and south-east of the county. Varied geological strata have provided a rich source of building material throughout Wiltshire, and include the well known Chilmark Stone, Portland Stone and the Oolitic limestone which has provided England with some of its finest stone.

Probably because of lack of water and possibly because of a change in climate, man gradually came down from his high downland home to the more fertile valleys where the greensand intersects the chalk, giving rise to numerous streams and rivers. The downs were left to the sheep which for a thousand years have grazed on the short turf and provided Wiltshire with a steady income. In the valleys and along the banks of the rivers, communities thrived and the springline villages of Wiltshire came into existence.

Although books have been written describing the whole of Wiltshire, very often authors have turned their attention to one particular village or area, finding variety, individuality and independence in the people. It is interesting to note while reading of the tremendous hardship encountered, especially in Victorian times, that time and time again people are said to have lived to a great age. In a delightful little book called *In a Wiltshire Valley* by Mrs Haughton published in 1879, the author describes life at that time in the Vale of Pewsey, hoping to record a way of life that was changing as rapidly as ours appears to be doing. In the book, she writes:

> The women in our valley worked in the fields as regularly as the men, and there must have been a strange fascination in the life, for those who once took to it never settled down again to indoors work. It is a very hard life, especially for the young girls, and at a very early age the women looked prematurely worn and haggard. Still, whether it was the result of passing so much of their time in the keen bracing Wiltshire air that counteracted the effects of hard work, scanty food, and insufficient apparel, certain it is that our old people, both men and women, lived to a very great age, many being nearer ninety than eighty at the time of their death.

The book is written with humour and insight, and is worth searching out. It has been reprinted by the Wiltshire Folk Life Society, and is described as a 'tiny masterpiece...a picture of the poor in the 1840s...when wages were low and a series of wet harvests brought hunger and hardship to rural workers.'

Alfred Williams deplored the passing of age-old, traditional ways of village life and saw industrial progress as a threat to the things he held so dear. He wrote widely on the characters around him, mentioning their robustness and age:

> ..up at four or half-past in the morning, strong and hardy, cheerful, vigorous and optimistic. Their shoulders were broad, their bellies round, their legs short and stout, their faces round too, robust and red, and jovial-looking; not pinched and thin, haggard and ghastly, like the townsfolk... Every member of the family was hardy and industrious. Did not Granny Bowles and Patty Titcombe, and Betsy Horton spend their whole lives, till they were nearly eighty, at work in the fields? and was any woman more robust and healthy, physically fit and vigorous

than they? Or can you imagine any more strongly principled and virtuous.

John Aubrey lived in the seventeenth century and his eye for detail and pleasure in the countryside and indeed his irritation with eccentricities are brought to us in a vivid and natural way. The minds of these authors seem to have been uncluttered by other pressures of life, so that, fortunately for us, they had a great capacity to write the details which make history a reality.

This book is not crammed with historical detail. It is an introduction to some of Wiltshire's most attractive and interesting villages which may encourage the visitor to look more closely. A good way to obtain a rudimentary knowledge of the places visited is to buy and collect the leaflets which are provided in most churches. They describe the church, its architecture and the associated prominent people, and often give a potted history of the village. Some villages, such as Heytesbury and Great Durnford sell booklets describing not only their particular church but those of the surrounding area, including occupations and much historical detail.

Bell turret, Biddestone

Almost every village in Wiltshire has particular features of interest especially to its inhabitants but of course not every village can be mentioned. Those chosen are through personal knowledge; I apologise now to those who feel left out. Some places have notable personalities which I have dwelt on, such as the creator of the wonderful garden at Stourhead; some have a particularly beautiful church, such as Edington or Steeple Ashton, which deserve more than a mention. Others are famous in their own right, such as Castle

Combe, or Lacock with its splendid Abbey and village owned entirely by the National Trust. Some are remote, but so attractive they must not be missed. Almost all have new estates or modern housing attached to them, but most retain their charm, their church, their manor house and their peace.

The craft of the thatcher is not dying, nor is the art of dry-stone walling. The recent interest in repairing and restoring instead of destroying for newer housing is apparent, and everywhere there is pride in living in a Wiltshire village. The gardens of both large and small houses are a joy, and where possible gardens that are open to the public in a particular area are mentioned. Many of the days out take a circular route which passes through villages by way of small scenic roads. Others, such as Stourhead, involve one place and its owners. If you embark on all the tours, this book will take you the length and breadth of one of the most unspoilt and underrated counties in England.

Margaret Wilson

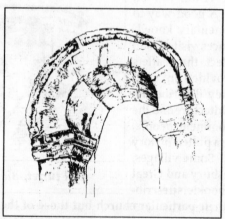

Saxon Arch, St Mary the Virgin,
Limpley Stoke

THE BRISTOL AVON

The source of the Bristol Avon is in the north-west corner of Wiltshire, the river gathering its waters from the foothills of the Cotswolds. It passes through Malmesbury, Chippenham and Melksham on its southward journey, and with increased volume turns west at Bradford on Avon before entering the Limpley Stoke valley. At Freshford it is joined by the River Frome and flows through the Warleigh valley to Bath. It receives the river Chew at Keynsham, and becomes tidal near Bristol before it passes under the Clifton suspension bridge to flow into the Severn at Avonmouth. West of Malmesbury the Avon is little more than a wide, shallow, peaceful stream enhancing many a small village on its way. The fine stone villages in this north corner of Wiltshire are the result of the flourishing wool trade of the medieval centuries, helped by particularly good building stone found in the region. This is an area somewhat forgotten by those intent on visiting the Cotswold heartland further north in Gloucestershire, although some eighteen villages in this part of Wiltshire are included in the officially designated Cotswold Area of Outstanding Natural Beauty.

Tour 1: Villages of the Upper Avon

At **Easton Grey** the Avon has 70 more miles to run as it passes under the ancient stone bridge in this attractive Cotswold village. Near the bridge is an old and beautiful house with gardens that touch the river bank, and an old turreted stone boathouse. Climbing the hill above the river is a hotchpotch of ancient buildings and roofs. On the opposite hill upstream is **Easton Grey House**, a mellow Queen Anne manor house commanding superb views of the valley below. Housed in this building is the elegant shop of Peter Saunders, selling sophisticated country wear and the like. There is also a fern-filled garden

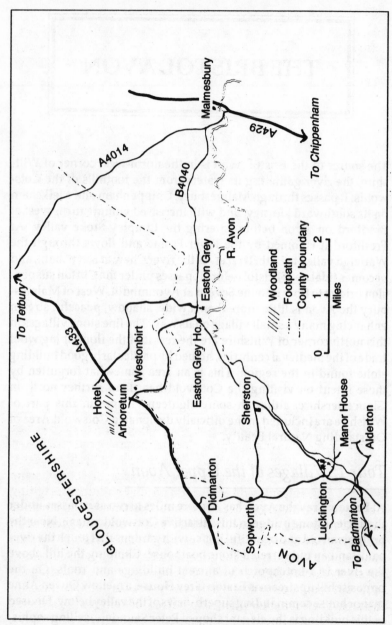

Tour 1: Villages of the Upper Avon

restaurant. In spring, daffodils line the curving drive to the house. The garden, which is open daily except Sunday (donations to the church; open for NGS in spring), is a place of beauty and tranquillity. The church, which was rebuilt in 1836, stands within the grounds of the house.

Easton Grey

Return to the B4040 and drive west along the valley past rich meadows where cows stand knee-deep in the slow ripples of water, and where, from any small bridge, fish can be seen in abundance.

The next village is **Sherston** with a wide High Street and some interesting seventeenth and eighteenth century buildings including the Angel Inn with its gables and mullioned windows. Sherston was built partly inside an ancient fortified earthwork, and the Roman Fosse Way passes within a couple of miles of the village. In 1016 the Danes under King Canute fought and lost a battle against Edmund Ironside. A local knight, John Rattlebone, was wounded during the battle but fought on bravely, and later was awarded the manor of Sherston. There is a somewhat dilapidated stone effigy of Rattlebone, thought to be a Norman representation, on the south side of the porch outside the church. Inside is an ancient chest with the initials RB,

'Rattlebone', Sherston church

which is supposed to be where Rattlebone kept his suit of armour.

The church is particularly lovely, having a late Norman arcade of four bays with decorated capitals of trumpet scallops and zigzags on the arches. The font is also Norman. The Early English crossing arches of the tower are a perfect example of that period as is the Early English window, with its detached Purbeck marble shafts and dogtooth decoration found in the north transept. The crossing arches rest on large carved heads which represent Simon de Montfort, Henry III and his Queen, and others including Ela, Countess of Salisbury — that remarkable woman who founded Lacock Abbey and Hinton Priory, and was High Sheriff of Wiltshire. On the south wall near the door there is a crucifix given to the people of Sherston by Italian prisoners of war who felt they had been treated kindly by the local inhabitants.

Opposite the church is the Rattlebone Inn with its neat and pleasant garden where one can sit for a drink and contemplate this lovely part of the world. On the other side of the road is the Sherston Wine Merchants, which specialises in Spanish wine. You may be lucky enough to join a wine-tasting session.

The road drops sharply and continues above the river until it approaches **Luckington**. This is a Cotswold village of good eighteenth century buildings. One is called the Pump House, and next to it is the former village lock-up. The village has an odd assortment of crossroads forming two village greens. As the road curves round into the village, take the sign to Alderton, and before the bridge in the valley you will see **Old Luckington** across the meadow. It is possible to open the gate and drive on the track to the church, but the walk of five minutes is pleasant. An enormous old cedar adds to the tranquil scene which includes the church, the faded apricot walls of Luckington Manor (open for NGS in Spring; also Luckington Court) a group of farm buildings and the lichen-covered walls and stone-tiled roofs of the rectory. The church of Our Lady and Ethelbert of Kent was built in the early thirteenth century with a nave with pointed arches and trumpet-scalloped capitals. The simple doorway is also thirteenth century, and so is the restored south chancel with its lancet windows and detached shafts of Purbeck marble similar to those at Sherston. The north wall has well-preserved scripts of the Lord's Prayer and creed which date from 1663. Behind the church a track descends to the Avon — a short and pleasant walk.

From the many signposts near the Green, find the narrow lane to **Sopworth**, another place of farms, church and manor house. The gardens of the Manor can be glimpsed through the main gate with a view of a stone-pillared pergola. This is a truly rural Cotswold village with some fine barns standing firm under the enormous weight of their stone-tiled roofs.

Where the lane meets the A433 turn right towards Tetbury, and soon you will reach **Westonbirt Arboretum** which is over the border in Gloucestershire. These famous acres of woodland, parkland, rides and walks were begun by Robert Holford in 1829 on open, agricultural land. For 63 years until his death in 1892 Robert Holford introduced and planted trees and shrubs from all over the world. The listed collection has now risen to over 10,500 specimens. It is well worth a visit in the spring to see its wonderful azaleas and rhododendrons and again in autumn when the place is afire with the colour of the turning leaves of the maples (open every day).

Westonbirt village is found south of the A433. Opposite the entrance to the Arboretum a small lane leads to the tiny Cotswold village of gabled cottages and pretty gardens. At the end of the lane is a golf course. The road south from the village returns to Easton Grey and Malmesbury.

Tour 2: The Flood Plain of the Avon

South of the M4 the Bristol Avon flows south across wide, open flood plains on its journey to Chippenham. To the south of the plain is the Tockenham/Bremhill ridge, a limestone formation known as Corallian. The stone, although not as compact as the excellent building stone around Box, is quarried and used locally, being similar to

Cotswold stone in appearance. Within these few square miles lived four authors of repute. North Wiltshire seemed to inspire the written word for not far away near Swindon, were born two more great authors — Richard Jefferies and Alfred Williams (*see* Tour 8).

Two antiquaries, John Aubrey (1626) and John Britton (1771) were born in the valley. Francis Kilvert the diarist was born at Hardenhuish (now a suburb of Chippenham) in the last century. Bremhill up on the ridge was the home of the poet/parson William Lisle Bowles, who was rector there for nearly 50 years.

Below the southern slopes of the ridge, the River Madden flows through lush green fields on its way to join the Avon near Chippenham. The course of the old railway between Chippenham and Calne runs close by, four miles of which have been turned into the Marden Nature Trail, noted for its varied fauna and flora.

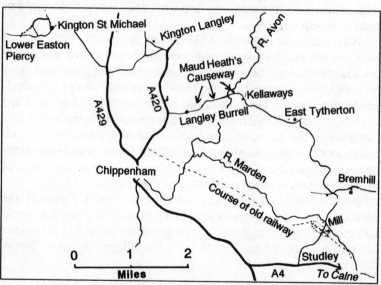

Tour 2: The Flood Plain of the Avon

Take the A4 south-east from Chippenham, turn left at Studley and look for the sign to **Bremhill**. The road passes over the Marden Nature Trail. Follow the road over the river near the mill and up the hill to the pub called Dumb Post Inn. From here there are spectacular views of the valley below, stretching to Calne and Cherhill Monument on the downs beyond. For a better view of the valley, leave the car and take the right of way to the left of the thatched house opposite the Dumb Post Inn sign. Fròm here it is a short walk across the top of the field to the church at Bremhill. What better way to approach this delightful ridge top village with its ancient church, village cross and pretty cottages!

The church of St Martin is thought to contain rare Anglo-Saxon work, namely long-and-short quoins in the north-west angle of the nave. Otherwise, it is chiefly a thirteenth century church undergoing much restoration in 1850. The late seventeenth century monument to George Hungerford has the arts of peace and war depicted by unusual instruments, cannons and pistols. Outside, large gargoyles bare their teeth from the crenellated parapet.

Close to the church is Bremhill Court, the former vicarage. William Lisle Bowles, an eccentric poet, was rector here between 1805 and 1844. Many of the churchyard inscriptions are his, and some of his now forgotten *Sonnets* ran to nine editions. His literary friends, among them Wordsworth, Charles Lamb and Tom Moore, would stand on his terrace discussing the urns, grottoes and stone monuments which he erected in the garden and listen to the sheep bells, which were tuned in thirds and fifths. Rector Bowles was a frequent visitor to Bowood (open to the public — *see* TIC), a few miles away, as he could be relied on to do something out of the ordinary; such qualities apparently made him a social asset.

Return to the car, and at the nearby crossroads go north to **Wick Hill** where there is a monument to Maud Heath erected by Bowles and the Marquis of Lansdown in 1838, with inscription by the poet. Maud lived at Langley Burrell, and peddled her wares each week in Chippenham. The road was frequently flooded, and was pitted and rutted, so in 1474 she set up a charity to build and maintain a causeway which ran four and a half miles from Wick Hill to Chippenham. The causeway was maintained and is still in use today, the most interesting section being at **Kellaways**, where the path is raised some six feet on stone arches as it crosses the Avon. On the road beside the Avon is a second monument telling of Maud and her generosity.

The road winds down the hill to **East Tytherton**, where a Moravian settlement was founded in 1745. There is an interesting group of buildings, the centre of which is a chapel, and attached to it are the Sisters' house and the Minister's house. Opposite are some pleasant houses, but the village hall, described by Pevsner as 'disastrous', is still there. (A house nearby called 'Kellaways' opens its gardens to

Maud Heath's Causeway

the public during summer: NGS and GS *see* Gardens Open).

Drive west to Kellaways and the arches of Maud's Causeway, and at **Langley Burrell** join the A420. Here Parson Kilvert, the diarist, helped his father while he was curate. Seek out the church among the park trees a little way north on the A420, as it has a Norman arcade and some Early English work. The school across the main road was built by Kilvert's great-great-grandfather. *Kilvert's Diaries* cover nine years between 1870 and 1879, giving a beautiful description of country life in Victorian times. His death from peritonitis in 1879, only five weeks after his marriage, was a tragedy.

Continue north taking the left turn to **Kington Langley**. Opposite the turn is the Greathouse (*c.*1700) with its nine-bay front - it is now one of the homes of the Cheshire Foundation. Kington Langley is all grass, with some interesting large houses among the trees. Continue to the A429 and cross it carefully, as it is the route to the motorway from Chippenham. Take the road to **Kington St Michael**. There is a good view of the church across the meadows as you approach the village. Turn left for the church, which is much restored, with Norman features. Both John Britton and John Aubrey were born nearby, and both are commemorated in the stained glass of a memorial window.

John Britton was born in the village of Kington St Michael in 1771.

At the age of 16 he went to London, where he tried his hand at a variety of things, which included compiling a songbook and contributing to a dramatic miscellany. He was subsequently asked to compile, with Edward Wedlake Brayley, *The Beauties of Wiltshire* (1801). The success of this led to 15 volumes of 'The Beauties of England and Wales' being produced between 1803 and 1814. While editing this, Britton is said to have travelled 3,500 miles.

John Aubrey's grandfather was Isaac Lyte, who became a London alderman. He gave to the village where he was born some fine almshouses for old people. They are known as the Lyte Almshouses and are found in the main street, a fine addition to any village.

Continue through the modern part of the village and turn left to **Easton Piercy**. John Aubrey was born in this hamlet in 1626. His education took place at Malmesbury, Blandford and Trinity College, Oxford. He entered the Middle Temple in 1646, but was never called to the Bar. On returning to Wiltshire, his interest in history, instilled into him by his grandfather, led him to be one of the first antiquaries to investigate Avebury. His romantic failures and lack of business sense caused him to lose most of his money through lawsuits, and much of his time was spent travelling from place to place. His association with the Oxford historian Anthony Wood and his interest in people and events gave rise to some biographical works, including some fine pen portraits in *Brief Lives*. One of the Brief Lives was autobiographical — much of it concerns the poor health and various accidents suffered by the author.

On the road to Easton Piercy a small turn to the right leads to **Priory Farm**, where parts of the Benedictine Nunnery, founded in 1155, have been incorporated into the present beautiful seventeenth century farmhouse. John Aubrey described the convent where the girls were educated by the nuns in many subjects including needlework, surgery, physic and drawing; he felt it was 'a fine way of breeding up young women'. There is a footpath across the fields here to Lower Easton Piercy — another splendid group of farm buildings. Return to Priory Farm by road (about 2 miles).

Tour 3 Lacock

At Chippenham the Avon flows due south, turns east near the agricultural college of Lackham (Open for NGS and GS; *see* Gardens Open) and south again to meander through lush meadows close by **Lacock Abbey**. The stream, which runs under the town bridge at Lacock before joining the Avon in the grounds of the Abbey, may have given Lacock its name, as the Saxon or Old English word for stream is *lacuc*.

After 1066 the two chief manors of the parish, Lacock and Lackham, were given to two Normans, Edward of Salisbury and William of Eu. Edward was the great-great-grandfather of Ela, Countess of

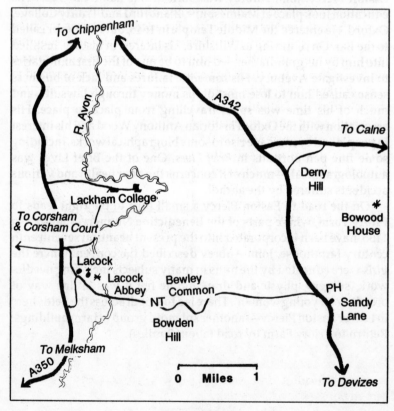

Tour 3: Lacock

Salisbury, who had married William Longspée, an illegitimate son of Henry II. He became Earl of Salisbury and was the first man to be buried in Salisbury Cathedral, having served three kings and spent much time away fighting in the wars. His relationship with his wife remained faithful and close, and when he was given up for dead while abroad, Ela had a dream that her husband would return to her. The dream came true – although William was to die shortly after, from the privations of war. Ela lived for another 35 years and founded Lacock abbey for Augustinian canonesses and became its Abbess. On the same day this remarkable woman found Hinton Priory for men some 15 miles away at Hinton Charterhouse.

The opening of a by-pass taking much of the traffic from Lacock has left its ancient streets and buildings in relative peace, and this beautifully preserved village with its fine Abbey is entirely under the jurisdiction of the National Trust. The medieval streets with examples of domestic architecture from many centuries are frequently turned into film sets: with the addition of an old cart, some straw on the ground and a few clucking hens, one is instantly transported to another time. The wide main street is ideal for festivities, and Morris dancers often entertain here. A hundred years ago a local doctor would play his fiddle while the young people danced.

Turn down narrow East Street past the fourteenth century tithe barn which once belonged to the Abbey estate, past the lock-up with its domed roof, past the little stone houses with their ancient tiled roofs, and turn into Church Street. To the left at the far end of the street is the early medieval construction of a cruck-framed house, and near to it the Angel Hotel with its hanging flower baskets adorning the stone-carved porch. The half-timbered buildings mix happily with the later Tudor and Georgian houses.

Lacock

At the other end of the street is the church of St Cyriac. It is a magnificent Perpendicular building, light and airy, with a wagon roof and a nave with clerestoried aisles. The transepts belong to the fourteenth century, although the south transept was rebuilt in Victorian times. There are some fine traceried windows, especially the very ornate east chancel window. Battlements and pinnacles adorn the church both inside and out, notably the Lady chapel which is decorated with delicate and beautiful carving. Remarkable tombs and tributes of unusual interest abound, the finest being the monument of Sir William Sharington, a man of somewhat dubious repute, whose fortunes turned when he came to live a Lacock Abbey in the sixteenth century. He died in 1553.

The Abbey (NT; *see* TIC) is situated in the meadows of the Avon, providing it with a natural and beautiful setting. The sacristy, the chapels, the chapter house and the cloisters are preserved from Ela's time, and in later centuries the Abbey has had many alterations and additions, notably during the ownership of Sir William Sharington who built a mansion around the nunnery in the Italian style of the 1500s. He also pulled down the church and built the fine stables. In the eighteenth century the Abbey was given a classical Palladian appearance, and this evolution of architectural styles blends well.

Ogee Arch, Lacock Abbey

The other famous name in Lacock's history is Talbot, to which is attached a romantic story. William Sharington's niece Olivia was courted by John Talbot, brother of the Earl of Shrewsbury. The young lovers met in secret, as her father disapproved of the liaison. One night in true Romeo style he was standing on the lawn of the abbey church and she on the battlements. She offered to leap down, and jokingly he encouraged her. She did indeed jump, and fell on John, who was knocked unconscious; but the episode so impressed her father that when John recovered he allowed them to marry. Two hundred years later, William Fox Talbot lived at the Abbey and became a famous pioneer of photography; his first successful picture, taken in 1835, features the oriel window in the long gallery.

The sixteenth century barn near the gates of the Abbey was opened as a **Museum of Photography** (NT; *see* TIC) in 1975, to commemorate Fox Talbot and his work, and visitors can see his first camera and calotypes, and the international awards that he won. The museum bookshop has an extensive range of books on photography.

The Avon and its meadows are crossed by a series of arched bridges, and the road winds up the hill to Bewley Common, a piece of land owned by the National Trust, where it is possible to park and picnic with the advantage of spectacular views over Wiltshire and beyond. In a couple of miles the road joins the A342 at **Sandy Lane**. Opposite is the George Inn; it is just one of the rather special buildings in this community of particularly pretty houses scattered along a busy road which, regrettably, is neither sandy nor a lane. A walk down one side of the road and back on the other gives an opportunity for photographing these chocolate-box buildings with their layers of thatch and perfect English cottage gardens.

North of Sandy Lane and hidden behind its acres of woodland is eighteenth century **Bowood House** (open to the public: *see* TIC) and its park designed by Lancelot Brown. The entrance to the rhododendron garden is a short way up the road from Sandy Lane, and parking is in a field on the right. The entrance to the house and grounds, including a particularly innovative children's playground, is at Derry Hill, a mile further on.

Tour 4: The Limpley Stoke Valley

The village of **Limpley Stoke** is scattered amongst the trees of a steep hillside above the Avon as the river winds through its magnificent valley on its way to Bath. In the shadow of its wooded hill the village had beginnings as a Roman settlement, and excavations have revealed the foundations of a Roman villa, earthworks, and many

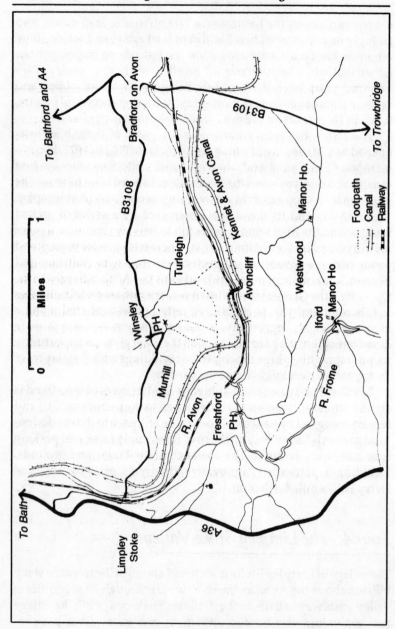

Tour 4: The Limpley Stoke Valley

artifacts. More is known of the Saxon settlement which followed. The ancient church of St Mary is found on the hill at the far end of the village, and its position is explained as follows in the Shaston Chartulary of 1322.

The Saxon builders of the early eleventh century 'commenced to build a church in a field down in the valley called Crockfords on the east side of the river, but that every night the Devil, or some other ghostly form, came and removed the stones to the top of the hill. After persevering for some days the builders resolved to use the site thus appointed'. The Devil in question can be seen as a sculpture above the font in the nearby church of Westwood. Whether or not he removed the stones, records show that 'an old Saxon Chapel of at least 280 years of age existed in a hamlet known as Hanging Stoke in 1349'.

The Saxon evidence in this remarkable little building is a rounded arch which forms part of the nave. It is a surprise to pass through the Norman doorway and, in the middle of the church, be confronted by this splendid stone archway. This was obviously the entrance to the Saxon Church, and could be locked from the inside by a strong bar, providing a place of refuge. The church was probably 'built about 1001 AD and was one of the Pear Tree Churches (there were seven in all) built to mark the position of a boundary pear tree which had been planted by the Abbess of Shaftesbury to mark the limit of her land' (from *The Visitor's Guide* in the church).

When the weavers came in the 1400s the village grew quickly and spread down the valley. Limpley Stoke now consists of Middle and Lower Stoke, and Upper Stoke (the part above the Warminster Road). If you walk down the lane opposite the church through Middle Stoke, you will see the weavers' cottages which in some cases have been modernised, but all retain their charm. The Rose and Crown has an interesting history and may date back to the sixteenth century.

The name 'Rose and Crown' was given to the earliest public houses to celebrate the end of the Wars of the Roses, though this building is more likely to be of seventeenth century origin. It began as a beer and cider house, but gradually changed to a 'house selling cider', and must have been a boon to travellers when the new Warmisnter road opened in the 1830s, when it also served teas. In 1964 it was modernized, and now has a restaurant overlooking the valley. Near the Rose and Crown, clear water flows from a recess in the wall. For many years this was one of the village wells and a favourite meeting place for people who had carried their buckets for up to a mile from their dwellings.

Historically, Lower Stoke is even more fascinating, for here excavations have provided possible evidence of an ancient reservoir belonging to a long-gone monastery. The Hop Pole Inn has walls dating from the 1300s and was used by monks on their journey to Bradford on Avon from nearby Hinton Priory when their trade was wool. There is supposed to be a secret tunnel from the inn to the river which was used by the monks at night.

Behind and above the Limpley Stoke Hotel is a well-tended, steeply-terraced children's playground. From here there are excellent views of the valley below. The playground was once part of the grounds of the hotel when it was a famous spa in the eighteenth century, making use of the vast network of natural fresh water-springs in the hillside. The West of England Hydropathic Establishment boasted all the latest treatments including Turkish baths, and was surrounded by acres of lovely gardens with waterfalls. (For information on Limpley Stoke I am indebted to Richard Hooker's local history project compiled in 1976/77 while he was still at school).

The lower road winds through the village to **Freshford** and emerges at the bridge which takes the road over the river Frome. Here, near The Inn at Freshford, is a pleasant walk across the meadow to the confluence of the Frome and the Avon. Continue up the wooded hillside opposite. Near the top a right-hand fork points the way along the Frome valley to Iford. Alternatively, continue on the main road to Westwood.

Iford is found at the end of a narrow lane where the Frome flows under an ancient bridge topped by a stone statue of Britannia. Nearby is Iford Manor with its attractive Italianate gardens forming a charming group. The gardens are open to the public on five afternoons a week in summer (*see* TIC). The steep hill climbs back to join the Westwood road.

Westwood stands along a high ridge and has much modern housing. Standing apart from the main village is the church of St Andrew's with its superb tower modelled on the central tower of Wells Cathedral. The east window contains some renowned stained glass from the fifteenth century. Over the wall is Westwood Manor, built in the fourteenth century and owned at one time by a well known clothier, Thomas Horton, who did so much for the cloth industry at Bradford on Avon. The Manor is owned by the National Trust and is open two or three times a week in summer (*see* TIC).

At the end of the village the road bears left to the historic small town of Bradford on Avon (Tourist Information Centre). On the Bath road out of Bradford look for the sign on the hill to Turleigh and its neighbouring village of Winsley. **Turleigh** is of mellowed stone tucked into the hillside above the Avon, and has seen little recent development.

Winsley Church

Winsley has seen more than its fair share of new housing, but somehow retains its ancient village heart. The old village is a hotch-potch of ancient cottages, farm buildings and barns, converted now to residential use but retaining their charm. In times past they were part of the Manor Estate which was included in the Shaftesbury Abbey Estate. The Manor itself is dated 1612, but many of Winsley's mellowed stone buildings are older, particularly Manor Farm near the War Memorial, which is said to date from the fourteenth century.

A walk through the old village is rewarding. Leave the car near the church of St Nicholas with its interesting Perpendicular tower having a rare saddleback roof. The rest of the building dates from 1841 and is joined to the tower by a small arch. Take the winding lane through the village, past cottages from the seventeenth, eighteenth and nineteenth centuries, and out to the main road. Turn left past the Sutcliffe School with its date 1657 when it was a farm. Round the corner is the recently restored village pub, the Seven Stars. In 1734 the landlord was wealthy enough to buy Burghope, the fine Elizabethan house at the south end of the village. The road, which takes a right turn near the bowling green, leads the walker past Winsley Manor to the end of the lane where the village cricket pitch has far-reaching views to the downs and the White Horse at Westbury.

For a longer walk continue down either of the tracks found here, both of which plunge down the hill to the river at Avoncliff and the newly restored section of the Kennet and Avon Canal. From here it is possible to walk to Bradford on Avon along the towpath and return to Winsley by bus.

NORTH-WEST WILTSHIRE

If a line were drawn diagonally from Swindon to Warminster the land to the south and east would be mainly chalk downland. The contrast between the chalk down and clay vale gives rise to the Wiltshire proverb 'as different as chalk from cheese' and indeed the manufacture of cheese in the north-west of Wiltshire was for centuries one of the county's great industries, Marlborough being a famous cheese centre for the London market. The other important source of wealth was weaving based on the large-scale grazing of sheep on the surrounding hills. Wool provided the money for the magnificent churches and buildings in the area; the oolitic limestone formation yielded those great blocks of freestone known as Bath Stone to provide the building material. The chief quarries were around Box and Corsham which from Roman times have produced the finest quality stone.

Across this land of farms and farming communities the Romans had laid part of their Fosse Way which ran from Lincoln to Exeter. A fine section of this ancient route, which is still in use today, runs from Batheaston north towards Sherston and beyond. At North Wraxall, Box and Atworth, Roman villas of note have been discovered and at Nettleton a military site was built c.AD 47 which later developed into a religious centre.

Across this land too came pilgrims en route for Glastonbury in Somerset. Their journey was made easier by hospices which gave them shelter. Chapels at Ditteridge, Chapel Plaister and South Wraxall still bear witness to those pilgrimages.

Tour 5: Castle Combe and Biddestone

Castle Combe is situated in the north-west of Wiltshire some 10 miles west of Chippenham and just south of the M4. It is found in a

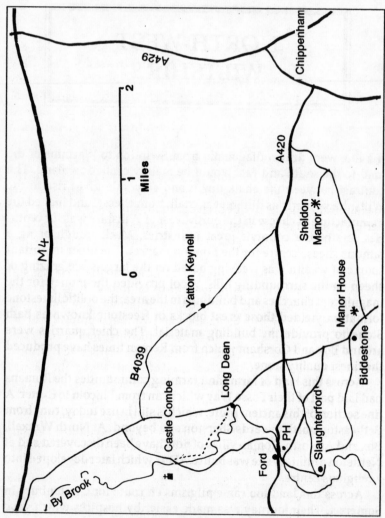

Tour 5: Castle Combe and Biddestone

valley beside a tributary of the Avon called the By Brook. Its name is derived from the valley or combe in which it was established and from the hilltop castle nearby, an ancient fortified earthwork which was used and probably enlarged by the Romans and then by the Saxons as a strategically important base for routing the Danes in the area. After the Norman Conquest the castle was rebuilt in the twelfth century and Reginald de Dunstanville, son of Henry I, was created Baron of Castle Combe.

Since 1962 **Castle Combe** has had the reputation of being England's 'prettiest village'. This accolade led in turn to the village being chosen as the location of 20th Century Fox's production of 'The Story of Dr Doolittle' in 1966. The resulting hordes of visitors have not diminished, and even on winter weekends it is the chosen spot for an outing. Parking in the village is scarcely allowed, and an extended visit to the village means a walk down the steep hill from the car park. Another more agreeable approach is by planning the day and walking up the valley from the south, leaving the car at Long Dean. The path runs along the side of the hill above the By Brook which meanders through its combe of steep woods and lush meadows. The perfect position of this most lovely of villages can be appreciated as the church tower and stone-tiled roofs gradually come into view through the trees.

The path emerges to cross the river at the lower village bridge, and it is a short walk to the pack bridge with its famous view up the main street of exquisite medieval domestic architecture. The cottages of mellowed limestone with their gables and dormer windows lead the eye up to the market cross with its stone-tiled pyramidal roofs and ancient beams. Of all the buildings, the Market Cross gives the most insight into a past way of life. Here was the focal point of the village, the hustle and bustle of the market which was held weekly on Mondays. A sheep fair on St George's Day which, after the decline of the wool trade was held on May 4th, continued as the Annual Fair until 1904. All the fun of the fair was there including swings, roundabouts, side-shows, cattle and sheep pens and traders shouting their wares.

The greater part of Castle Combe's development was due to the wool trade. By the thirteenth century there may have been an established cloth trade for it is possible that the Romans, who had knowledge of spinning, weaving, fulling and dyeing, introduced these crafts to the area. In Domesday at least three nearby mills are mentioned, although no doubt they were mainly used for grinding corn. By the fourteenth century the village began to take the shape we know today, particularly under the guiding hand of Sir John Fastolf, lord of the manor. This was the man on whom it is said Shakespeare modelled his famous 'fat knight', the immortal Falstaff in his play Henry IV, although the portrayal was somewhat inaccurate. Sir John

Castle Combe

Fastolf was a larger than life character who spent much time in France doing battle. Castle Combe seems to have escaped the general unrest found elsewhere in the country at that time, and with a thriving wool trade it prospered greatly. Although Sir John was abroad a great deal, his thoughts were with the village, and he purchased the market and fair, and also bought his tenants the privilege of freedom from certain taxes under the Royal Seal. Several mills and many cottages were erected for Sir John's workers, and for 22 years he supplied his soldiers overseas with the famous red and white cloth called Castle Combe which he bought from the mills. It was a time of great industry, and the high land in the neighbourhood provided much wool and also wheat and barley.

The church of St Andrew became a tribute to the weaving industry and the growing village population. During the fifteenth century the church, with its thirteenth century beginnings, was enlarged. It is chiefly Perpendicular in appearance, with a fine chancel arch with canopied statuettes of saints. The tower was built in 1436, its buttresses decorated with shafts and pinnacles and its top with battlemented arches. In the last century the church was found to be unstable and, except for the tower, the thirteenth century chancel east wall and part of the north chapel with its lovely Decorated traceried windows was pulled down and rebuilt in 1850.

In medieval times the Manor House consisted of a large hall and gallery, one or two chambers and a stable. The park was stocked with deer which on occasion the tenants were allowed to kill. In the early days Fastolf had venison sent to him in Hampton, where he lived during 1411-12. At this time the Manor was divided into housing for the tenants, and it is not until 1645 that mention is made of further extensions and additions such as the dairy, buttery, wool loft, oxhouse and wagon house. The old entrance hall of 1664 with its dark oak panelling is preserved to this day. In the period 1830-50 the whole building was 'brought up to date' by the Victorians, and additions were made by Edward Lowndes who had purchased the estate. He took great interest in the property and laid out gardens, planted the splendid trees and created carriage drives of some 10 miles in length through the woods. Lowndes was also responsible for the kitchen garden and fine drive with its iron gates which bear his initials. During the last war the Manor was turned into a hospital, and in 1949 it was sold again, to be converted to a residential country hotel, which is internationally known today. Another wartime enterprise, the airport to the north of the village, has now been turned into a popular car and motor-cycle racing track.

Return by foot to **Long Dean** or drive south to the A420. Turn right and immediately left to cross the By Brook at **Ford**, where refreshment can be found at the White Horse Inn with its appealing riverside garden. Follow the signs through the lanes to Biddestone.

Another Cotswold village of great charm, **Biddestone** has a wide village centre with an attractive duck pond, and is almost as popular with visitors as its neighbour Castle Combe. It has some superb architecture and fine houses, including the Manor at the south end of the village. The house is not open to the public, but the garden is opened once a year (NGS) and is well worth a visit. Biddestone once had two churches and the remaining one, St Nicholas, has an unusual thirteenth century stone bell turret and a plain Norman doorway with a Maltese cross above, and in the chancel Norman windows. St Peter's was demolished some years ago, but its bell turret resides on the lawn of the Manor Hotel in Castle Combe.

At the south end of the village turn left for **Sheldon Manor**, a couple of miles away from Chippenham. The Manor is all that remains of a medieval village, and has recently opened its thirteenth century door and acres of superb gardens to the public (*see* TIS). The Manor is also signposted from the A420.

Tour 6: Villages east of Bath

The large village of Box sits astride the A4 half way between Bath and Chippenham. There are good views to the north, and down in the valley the By Brook is on its way to join the Avon. High on the other side of the valley is **Colerne** with its lofty church tower as its landmark. Colerne is a Cotswold village with an airfield on the flat plateau to the north and splendid panoramic views. The church, with its Perpendicular tower, is known for its Saxon treasure — pieces of a ninth century cross shaft with interlaced carving. The village can be reached from Box along a very narrow lane passing close to the small hamlet of **Ditteridge** with its thatched cottages and farms and simple Norman church with an Early English chancel. Nearby was a Georgian spa that had a pump room and a boarding house. Spa House still stands and was perhaps the boarding house.

Box found fame during the eighteenth century building boom when Bath's magnificent buildings were erected. Legend has it that long before that time St Aldhelm discovered this most famous stone of the Great Oolite formation, and it is still known as St Aldhelm Box Stone, or, more familiarly, as Bath Stone. The quarries, which are still in production, also yielded the stone for the Box Tunnel on the old GWR line, one of Brunel's greatest engineering feats in the last century. The splendid entrances to the tunnel show a great Victorian pride. The tunnel itself is 3,212 yards in length.

The area around Box was favoured by retired Roman officers who built their villas close to the road which ran from Bath to Mildenhall in the east of the county. One large villa, 100 yards north-west of the church, was excavated in the last century and was found to have 40 rooms, several of which lay above hypocausts providing steam heating for a bath suite. Some of the rooms had mosaic floors still visible today.

The church of St Thomas of Canterbury is fourteenth century with fine Decorated traceried windows and a central spired tower. The south aisle was added in 1840 and dedicated to the navvies who worked on the tunnel. It is found below the main road, and is surrounded by a churchyard full of fine table tombs. This old part of

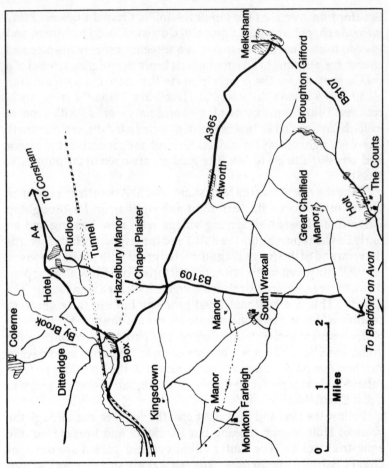

Tour 6: Villages east of Bath

the village includes the mullion- windowed Old School now called Springfield House. Back in the main street is the village lock-up, with a domed stone roof. The seventeenth century Manor Farmhouse stands a little incongruously wondering what happened to its countryside setting. The Victorian school has an extraordinary, spindly tower.

Drive east on the A4 noting Brunel's tunnel entrance on the right. At the top of the hill turn right on to Leafy Lane beside Rudloe Park Hotel. Follow the signs to Bradford Road and turn right towards

Bradford on Avon. At the top of the hill is **Chapel Plaister**, a tiny wayside chapel, amongst a group of Cotswold stone buildings, and easy to miss. The little chapel was a fifteenth century hospice and church for pilgrims to Glastonbury; it bears the pilgrim symbol of a cockle shell above the door. Opposite the chapel, a footpath sign leads down a long driveway to Hazelbury Manor, a large, well-restored Tudor house containing its original great hall with a roof of 'collarbeams on arched braces and two tiers of wind-braces' (Pevsner). There is a right of way for walkers through the grounds of the manor and across the fields to Box. The gardens are open to the public (*see* NGS).

Take the A365 towards Melksham, and at **Atworth**, the site of an important Roman villa, turn right and right again for **Broughton Gifford**, a pleasant, straggling village with new housing and an Early English church. Join the B3107 and turn right for **Holt**. Towards the west end of this long village there is a green with pleasant houses. Around the green to the left is the Victorian church with a Perpendicular tower. Before reaching the green, look for a sign saying 'The Courts'. This is a National Trust property built in the eighteenth century where the local magistrate sat to adjudicate in the disputes of the weavers in the cloth industry. The gardens surrounding the house are a haven of peace, and are open to the public most days in summer (*see* NGS). Opposite the garage and the Toll Gate pub, resplendent in summer with flowers and hanging baskets, is a sign to Great Chalfield.

Follow the lane and turn right past the conifers and through the gates of Holt Manor, looking out for riders and horses from the equestrian centre. The Tudor chimneys and gabled windows of **Great Chalfield Manor** (open 3 days a week in summer; *see* TIC) can be glimpsed across the fields. This approach leads over the stream near a sluice gate. Water from the stream feeds a moat round this superb fifteenth century manor house which belongs to the National Trust. Its position amid the flat surrounding countryside is a surprise, for here is one of the most important Tudor manor houses in the country. Thomas Tropnell built it in 1480; it was restored in this century and is open to the public, usually on one day in the week only. The Church, which is contemporary with the house, is approached through the gatehouse of the manor.

An avenue, flanked by staddle-stones, leads away from the house. Drive down the avenue, and follow the lane to the T-junction.

Great Chalfield

Turn left and left again at the next T-junction, following the sign to **South Wraxall**. At a five-lane junction take the South Wraxall lane on the right. The village has a church with a tower from the thirteenth century. The tower has a saddle-back roof, and this is repeated on the square stair-turret. The Long family had a hand in part of the building of the church, and inside is a large monument to Thomas Long, 1759, and his wife, 1733. Making an attractive group near the church are Church Farmhouse, late seventeenth century with five bays and a hipped roof, the Long Arms Inn and the school of 1841.

In the vicinity, about a mile north of the village, is another important medieval house – South Wraxall Manor. This dates from the fifteenth century, the gatehouse and great hall being from that time. Later parts are Elizabethan and Jacobean. It was begun by Robert Long about 1430, and is no longer owned by the family. It is not open to the public and all one can do is stand and stare at the outside of this magnificent building set among well-mown gardens. The farmhouse nearby is earlier, and was a fourteenth century hospice for travellers. Non-smokers may be shocked to hear that it was in this exquisite house that Sir Walter Long and his friend Sir Walter Raleigh sat and smoked their pipes filled with a strange weed that Raleigh had brought back from his travels. It was thought to be

South Wraxall

the first time people had smoked in an English house.

Monkton Farleigh, a mile away to the west, has a Manor which used to be a Cluniac priory. It was founded in the twelfth century and few fragments of building remain. The main facade is nineteenth century, and stands at the top of a wide green mile-long ride, which leads to South Wraxall. In a field a little north of the Manor, a small fourteenth century stone structure known as the Monks' Conduit housed a spring which was the water supply for the Priory.

Halfway down the steep main street lined with stone cottages is the church of St Peter's. It has a Norman door and a thirteenth century tower, and inside is a particularly good example of linenfold panelling. Dominating the church is a big Victorian Gothic rectory with tall carved chimneys and leaded windows.

The road north from Monkton Farleigh leads back to Bath.

THE THAMES VALLEY

Between the towns of Swindon and Malmesbury, Wootton Bassett to the south and Cricklade to the north, there was a great forest known as Bradon Forest. Indeed, away from the chalk downs much of Wiltshire was covered by dense forests, many of them – Savernake, Chute, Clarendon, Cranborne Chase and others – became favourite royal hunting grounds of Norman and medieval kings. Bradon Forest once covered approximately 15,000 acres, and settlements such as Minety, Purton, Charlton, Lydiard Tregoze and Wootton Bassett (the 'wood' town of the forest) lay well within the woods. At Nath's Farm in Minety an oak tree with a girth of 28 feet is a survivor of Bradon Forest. An Ordnance Survey map of the area shows clearly the extent of deforestation, although a few large areas of woodland exist such as Fisteridge Wood near Oaksey and Pond Plantation south of Minety which borders Bradon Pond. (The road which runs through the wood does not allow public access to the lake.)

Around the Fosse Way in the foothills of the Cotswolds rise the streams which form the headwaters of the Thames. One would be forgiven for thinking that Swillbrook, which is joined by Derry Brook from the south and forms the border of the old forest, is indeed the Thames river. However it is the tiny stream which flows under the many little stone bridges of Ashton Keynes which is known as Isis or Thames. At Cricklade, the river is more distinguishable as it flows north along the Wiltshire/Gloucestershire border before entering Oxfordshire.

Tour 7: Ashton Keynes and nearby villages

From Malmesbury take the A429 to **Crudwell** where the thirteenth and fifteenth century church with Norman beginnings is flanked by a fine group of stone buildings. Here is a buttressed fifteenth century

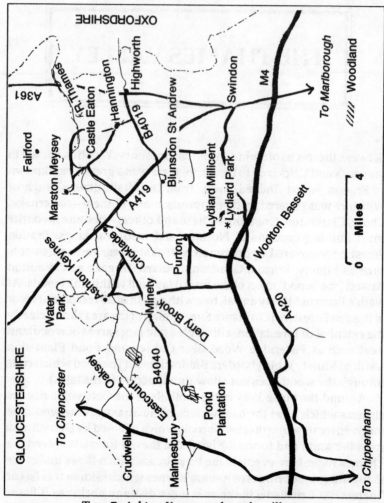

Tour 7: Ashton Keynes and nearby villages

barn, the Old Rectory from the seventeenth and eighteenth centuries with a circular dovecote, and the School House of 1670 which was once half school and half the master's house, and is now private dwellings. To the west is Crudwell Court, a Georgian building with a pedimented porch with Tuscan columns. Past the church, the stream forms a pond before the road leaves the village signposted to Oaksey.

The straggling village of **Oaksey** has some interesting seventeenth century stone cottages and farmhouses amongst some drab modern and Victorian architecture. To the north at Dean Farm are the remains of a motte-and-bailey Norman castle known as Norwood Castle. The church is entered under a particularly good example of a fourteenth century ogee arch, and has a thirteenth century arcade. The walls have fragments of texts and paintings, one of which is The Christ of the Trades, showing Christ surrounded by tools, with the moral that salvation is in labour.

Frequent signs on the road to Ashton Keynes direct the visitor to the **Cotswold Water Park**, a large area of man-made lakes derived from gravel pits which have been put to good use in providing every water sport imaginable. We visited it in winter and spent some time skimming stones long distances across its frozen wastes. Situated so far from the sea, this enterprise is sure to be popular with local inhabitants, particularly from the ever-growing town of Swindon.

Ashton Keynes is a delightful place and it is worth walking around its lanes to appreciate its attractive stone architecture, the little bridges over the infant Thames and its flower-bedecked gardens. Seek out Church Walk with its eighteenth century stone houses. Here, where the stream widens, Ashton Mill and Brook House are of particular merit. Ashton Keynes provided hospitality in the 1930s for a group of pacifists known as the Cotswold Bruderhof, many of whose members were refugees from Germany and other European countries which had totalitarian governments. They formed a community in the area, living on a 300-acre farm and dressing in medieval peasant costume. The coming of the war saw them emigrate to Paraguay.

East and north of Cricklade a finger of Wiltshire penetrates the Gloucestershire countryside almost as far as Fairford. In this finger, in the meadows north of the young Thames, lies the little village of **Marston Meysey** with stone cottages forming its one long street, and several good seventeenth century houses with barns. The derelict Round House, situated near a hump-bridge, was one of several canal houses built along the Thames and Severn Canal.

South of Marston Meysey, by way of **Castle Eaton** and **Hannington** with its Elizabethan mansion, is **Highworth**. It stands, as its name suggests, on a ridge with a splendid view of the vale. A cannon-ball from the Civil War is preserved in the church, which it struck. From Highworth, keeping north of Swindon, travel west on the B4019.

The Thames, Ashton Keynes

Cross the A419, taking the road to **Blunden St Andrew** with its dramatic nineteenth century Blunden Abbey, now in ruins, and continue to the B4041, the Cricklade-Wootten Bassett road.

Turn left for **Purton**. The church at Purton has the unusual distinction of having both a tower and a spire built at different periods. In Saxon times the great battle of Ellandune took place here between Wessex and Mercia in 823. Purton has much to offer around its church, half-a-mile away from the High Street, where the brick chimneys of the stone manor house (from 1600), the Norman, Early English and Decorated Gothic church, and the timber barn with brick infilling, form a splendid picture.

A mile or so south of Purton, in an undulating and rural setting, is **Lydiard Millicent**, a large and attractive village with a church built in the fourteenth and fifteenth centuries and a Norman font. It lies by the parish of Lydiard Tregoze, the meaning of Lydiard being 'a pass between two hills'. The village of Lydiard Tregoze is no longer in existence, but Lydiard Park, a Georgian mansion owned by Swindon Corporation, is a conference centre and management school. The extensive grounds are open to the public. Here also is the parish church of St Mary, a little church full of colour and splendour and worthy of a visit.

North of Purton, and once in the centre of the forest, is **Minety**, its name derived from the mint which grows in its streams. Another long, straggling village, Minety's Victorian railway station lay one-and-a-half miles from the Perpendicular church of St Leonard. Among the many modern bungalows there are some buildings of interest.

In his book *An Acre of England*, L.J. Manners details the farms, houses and people known to him throughout his life, and writes delightfully of buildings such as Minety House, the home of Major C.C. Goldsmith from the beginning of the century. The Major organised the village cricket and was the first man in Minety to own a car, which he would drive at speed, bringing up clouds of dust on the rutted roads. Hovington House, near the church, stands on the site of the oldest house in the parish which, legend has it, was inhabited by priests who used an underground passage to the church. The Mansells is now the oldest building in the neighbourhood, a seventeenth century building with later additions, once the home of the Penn family who founded Pennsylvania in the USA. Return to Malmesbury on the B4040.

NORTH-EAST WILTSHIRE

In the last century Swindon was a village on the top of a hill with a postal address of 'Swindon, near Highworth'. Its growth was due initially to the Marquess of Ailesbury who adamantly refused to allow the Great Western Railway to lay its London to Bristol track through Savernake Forest. Swindon was proposed as an alternative, having the advantage of being close to the Wiltshire and Berkshire Canal which could carry coal and coke for the railway. Also its much more northerly position would provide a junction for a branch line to Gloucester and Cheltenham. Town Planning was simpler in those days – the site of the new railway works was chosen by 21-year-old Daniel Gooch, an apprentice in George Stephenson's workshop who became Superintendent of the GWR. He and his superior, I.K. Brunel, were sitting on a bank having a picnic lunch when Gooch threw a stone; where it fell a peg was inserted to mark the site of the first building.

The great Victorian railway works, which in 1867 covered 18 acres, have now been phased out although it is still a busy junction. In its turn the M4 has restored Swindon's fortunes providing a fast link with London and a gateway to the West and Wales. Its dramatic spread has made it one of the great commercial towns of England.

Tour 8: The Countryside south of Swindon

On a hill south of Swindon, sheltering beneath the downland escarpment, is the village of **Liddington** which gives its name to the Iron Age earthwork on the hill behind it. It is one of many small attractive villages within commuting distance of the ever-increasing town nearby.

Liddington is a refreshing place with splendid views. Curiously, its church is apart from the village and is found on the other side of

44

the busy main road. It was founded in the thirteenth century by an Abbess of Shaftesbury, whose tomb can be seen in the churchyard. The village has some attractive thatched cottages and an imposing manor house that can be glimpsed by walking down the public footpath signposted to Ham Road from The Street. This Elizabethan house has an ancient moat which has been enlarged as a garden pond. The footpath passes the entrance and is set in a glade of beeches with a gurgling brook. It is no more than a ten minute walk round the village and back to the car.

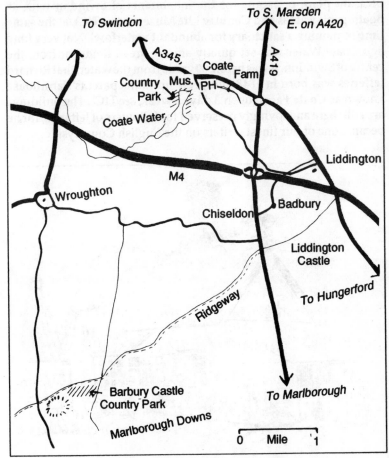

Tour 8: The Countryside south of Swindon

If you cross the main road again and take the small road opposite, you will see the signpost to Badbury. This road takes you over the motorway to **Liddington Hill**, a particularly worthwhile hill to climb for its magnificent views of the countryside and the univallate hill fort on its summit. There is also a plaque stuck somewhat ignominiously on the trig point in memory of Richard Jefferies, writer and naturalist. If you look down towards Swindon you will see the long length of **Coate Water**. It began life as a reservoir for the Wiltshire and Berkshire Canal, and is now the centre of a Country Life Park, a pleasant place of escape for the inhabitants of Swindon with its boating, play areas and Country Life Museum (*see* TIC), at the same time remaining a sanctuary for abundant waterfowl. Not very long ago Coate Water was set quietly among green fields far from the centre of Swindon. It was here, 200 yards from the water, that Richard Jefferies was born in 1848 and grew up in his parents' farmhouse known as **Coate Farm** (open 3 days a week; *see* TIC). The buildings are still there and lovingly preserved for followers of Jefferies, for he became one of our finest writers on the English Countryside.

Coate Farm, birthplace of Richard Jefferies

As a boy, Jefferies worked without much enthusiasm on his parents' farm. Times were hard and money scarce, and to avoid the frequent arguments at home Richard would spend much time walking the downs observing the natural things around him. Probably writing of Liddington Hill, he said:

> There was a hill to which I used to resort...the labour of walking three miles to it, all the while gradually ascending, seemed to clear my blood of heaviness accumulated at home...at every step my heart seemed to obtain a wider horizon of feeling. By the time I had reached the summit I had entirely forgotten the petty circumstances and annoyances of existence. I felt myself. I was utterly alone with the sun and the earth.

To the great relief of his parents, a chance meeting with a young reporter on the *North Wilts Herald* brought Richard his first job, and his observations and thoughts were transferred to paper. He contributed regular articles on the plight and character of the Wiltshire farmer, and wrote 20 books drawing heavily on places, people and things that he knew well. He immortalised Coate Water with his story of a boy called Bevis, whose imaginary adventures around the lake gave great insights into Jefferies' character. This detailed writing on such things as hunting or the harvest are unsurpassed, and his closeness to nature and feeling of oneness with the universe seemed to provide this great thinker with an insight into eternity.

For five years he fought a losing battle against tuberculosis, and died in Sussex in 1887 at the age of 38. In Salisbury Cathedral there is a marble bust of this remarkable writer inscribed to his memory.

Coate Farm is open to the public. In the tiny attic room, Jefferies' work and that of another Wiltshire writer are remembered. Alfred Williams was also a naturalist in whom Wiltshire takes great pride. Born in South Marston near Swindon, Williams spent much of his working life at the railway works, but like Jefferies, his spare time was spent walking the hills and feeling the fresh air and joy of the natural world about him. His greatness lay in his poetry, and although he was only 10 when Jefferies died, he must have felt a great affinity for him, and wrote of him in a poem.

Barbury Hill Fort is another great Iron Age camp on the Marlborough Downs, and together with 100 acres of open downland, **Barbury Castle Country Park** provides some spectacular views across

Sarsen Stone, Badbury Castle

the Vale of the White Horse, the undulating landscape looking like an enormous duvet of green and yellow hues. The approach to the hilltop from Wroughton is on minor roads which cross the Ridgeway before reaching the top, where there is a short walk to the fort. Before arriving at the car park, there is a gate on the left which leads to the side of the hill and to a large sarsen stone set as a monument to the two great writers.

> Alfred Williams
> 1877-1930
> Still to find and still to follow
> Joy in every hill and hollow
> Company in solitude

And on the other side facing his birthplace is the inscription:

> Richard Jefferies
> 1848-1887
> It is Eternity now
> I am in the midst
> of it. It is about
> me in the sunshine.

THE KENNET VALLEY

Tour 9: Avebury

We first visited **Avebury** (NT) on a sunny, sparkling winter's morning when the frost lay thick on the ground and the world was still. We ran up and down the ditches of Avebury Circle and hugged the great stones, feeling their antiquity and strength. Later in the year, daffodils danced near the green mounds, and lambs cavorted around the massive stones. On another occasion masses of cowslips grew from the green turf, apparently undeterred by countless visitors. Avebury is an experience no one should miss. It is a place of beauty and discovery, providing a feeling which is both humbling and rewarding.

Much has been written on Avebury's prehistoric monuments, and the Department of the Environment's official handbook, *The*

Avebury

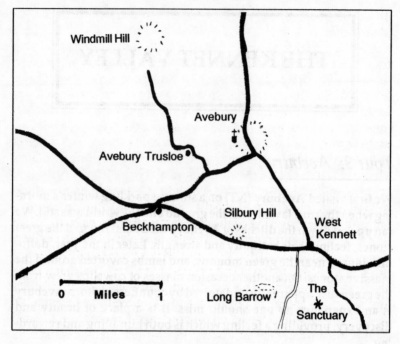

Tour 9: Avebury

Avebury Monuments, is particularly clear in describing Avebury Circle, the early Neolithic settlement called Windmill Hill, West Kennet Long Barrow, whose dark and eerie interior can be visited, and Silbury Hill, the largest man-made prehistoric mound in Europe, where from time to time excavations have been carried out, to reveal little more than the skeleton of a murdered traveller. West Kennet Avenue, which runs between Avebury and the Sanctuary, may have been built for semi-religious purposes. John Aubrey was the first to make a plan of this amazing complex in 1660 and it was investigated by William Stukeley and Richard Colt Hoare in the eighteenth century. Since then it has been well documented. As well as the Alexander Keiller Museum and the English Heritage Centre in the village, Devizes Museum houses a wealth of information on Avebury (Information on opening times; *see* Properties Open).

The **Avebury Circle**, which is the centre of a complex of prehistoric monuments, contains the historic components of the village of Avebury. The rest of the village is often forgotten, as it lies a little distance apart at **Avebury Trusloe**, the core of which is Trusloe Manor.

The church at Avebury is of great beauty and importance, dating back to the Saxon era. An investigation of the church reveals Saxon windows high up in the north wall, round-headed Saxon windows in the south wall, a carved south doorway from the twelfth century and a Norman font with cushion capitals, intersecting arches and an unusual representation of Christ trampling on dragons, a popular motif in the Middle Ages. The chancel, chancel arch and a lancet window in the west wall of the north aisle are late thirteenth century. The rood loft, carved in the West Country style, is from the fifteenth century, and is a rarity. In the sixteenth it was removed, perhaps following an order from Elizabeth I, and carefully hidden behind a lath and plaster covering against the east wall of the nave. In 1810 it was discovered and repainted. The tower is also fifteenth century. The present aisles date from 1810, and the oak pulpit is c.1840, having originally resided in the parish church of St Mary, Thatcham, Berkshire. So this church, which saw Saxon children baptised, has seen and taken advantage of the architectural innovations through the centuries. The round Saxon windows deserve more than a casual glance, for the method of insertion in a thick blank wall can be discerned. In order to place a stone window into a rubble wall, the Saxon builder devised a basketwork frame in which to set his plaster. The holes for the willow sticks that were used can still be seen around the window.

Behind the church is Avebury Manor, which dates from the 1550s I am delighted that this lovely building now belongs to the National Trust and is now open to the public (*see* TIC). Housed in its converted coach-house and stable is the Museum founded by the late Alexander Keiller in 1938 to display the finds from his excavations at nearby Windmill Hill. It also contains material from the West Kennet Long Barrow, the Sanctuary, Silbury Hill and Avebury itself.

The Wiltshire Folk Life Society was established in 1975 as an educational charity to develop public interest in the study of the social, domestic and economic history of Wiltshire. What better place for the display of exhibits and the demonstration of crafts than The Great Barn! One of the biggest and most expensive items in its restoration programme was the re-thatching, which provides an excellent example of the traditional skills of the thatcher. The barn has been open for several years and attracts many thousands of visitors

The Great Barn, Avebury

annually. There are regular demonstrations of crafts, including sheepshearing, hurdle-making, coopering, leatherwork, corn dollies, wood-turning and many others. Folk and Morris dancers often perform outside the barn.

Tour 10: Villages east of Marlborough

Between Marlborough and the Berkshire border, the Kennet River runs gently through a wide green valley, passing villages of half-timbered, thatched houses and old mellowed red-brick buildings standing side by side with more modern housing. Many buildings are of flint and stone, and contain flint decoration in their walls. There is tranquillity here, and between the villages wheat-fields line the roads and stretch away over the undulating hills.

Leaving Marlborough on the Ramsbury road, the first village in this pleasant countryside is **Mildenhall**, once the ancient Roman town of *Cunetio* – a centre of importance. From here Roman roads ran to Bath (*Aquae Sulis*) and Wanborough (*Durocornavium*). South-east of the village is the site of the Roman town where excavations have been carried out, to reveal a rectangular enclosure with streets, a village and a gateway with a paved entrance. St John the Baptist church spans all the architectural centuries, having Anglo-Saxon windows in the lower part of a tower finished by the Normans, Early English arches, Perpendicular windows and Late Georgian furnishings.

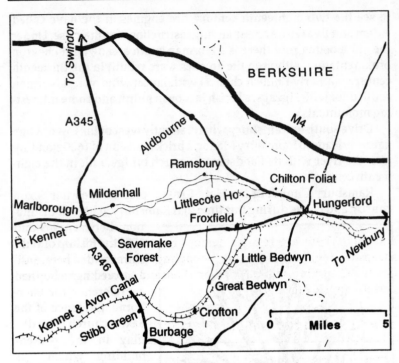

Tour 10: Villages east of Marlborough

Shortly after Axford, where Priory Farm on the banks of the river hides a fourteenth century chapel among its farm buildings, turn left for **Aldbourne**. This place, pronounced locally as 'auburn', contains all the ingredients of village life – a green with village cross, a duck pond, attractive houses and cottages of brick and thatch, a sixteenth century court house and an eighteenth century brick house with nine bays. The church, which dominates the green, dates back to Norman times with additions through the centuries to the present day.

Much history and tradition is attached to Aldbourne; the village was the subject of a book by Ida Gandy called *The Heart of a Village*. In the seventeenth and eighteenth centuries it was famous for its bell foundry, specialising in bells for animals, particularly horses. Two other industries were willow-plaiting and straw-plaiting, the former being popular for the decoration of fireplaces in summer and the latter for use in the millinery trade.

The church, with its Perpendicular tower, must be visited if only

53

to see the two eighteenth century fire engines in the nave called Adam and Eve with accompanying instructions for their use. Under the old wooden roof there is a Norman south arcade with chevron ornamentation, although the arcades were rebuilt in the thirteenth century, an Early English chancel with lancet windows, a Norman south door with zigzags, a lavish Jacobean pulpit and some interesting monuments.

Drive south to **Ramsbury** where, slightly west of the town, a fine gateway leads to Ramsbury Manor, a brick mansion of 1680 standing near the river with its handsome five-arch bridge built in the eighteenth century.

Ramsbury Church of the Holy Cross replaced an earlier Saxon church, and it was during this time that Ramsbury achieved distinction. Between 909 and 1058 the Bishop of Wiltshire resided here, until a succeeding bishop had a preference for Sherborne. Evidence of the Saxon church is on display in the present building, which was built of flint and stone and dates from the thirteenth century. It has many interesting features, including a most unusual font. Small children enjoy being lifted up for a glimpse of the fish carved inside the bowl. Immediately north of the church is Parliament House, one of the finest houses in the village and built in the late seventeenth century.

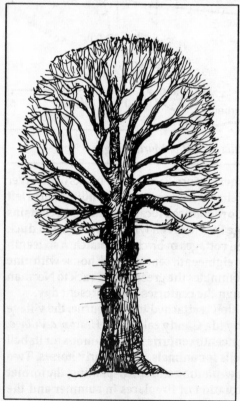

Ramsbury Elm

In the main street is The Malt Shovel, a pub

In the garden at Littlecote

with a riverside garden. The street broadens near the Bell Inn and in front of it stood the famous Ramsbury elm which was the logo of the old Ramsbury Building Society founded in 1846 and continued by its successor, the West of England Building Society. To replace the mighty elm which was destroyed by Dutch Elm Disease, the Society has recently (1986) planted a semi-mature oak tree, an event which was recorded on BBC Television National News. The original tree was a seedling in the time of King Charles I and nearly 130 years later John Wesley preached beneath it. The massive stump was removed in October 1986 amid much controversy in the village as to whether the tree was indeed dead. Local folklore has it that the village witch Maud Toogood made her home in the tree.

At the east end of the village there is a division of the ways. Take the right hand fork and cross the bridge to **Froxfield**. The road leads over the hills and drops down to the A4 near Froxfield's flintstone village church with its shingled bell tower. Turn left and left again beside the Duchess of Somerset's almshouses, built in the seventeenth century, and continue along the narrow road towards Littlecote House. Littlecote can also be approached from Ramsbury by way of **Chilton Foliat** from where the great house can be seen across the Kennet water meadows.

This is an attractive village of Georgian houses amid timbered cottages. The flint and stone church dates from the thirteenth century and notable is the eighteenth century rectory nearby. A short distance away is Chilton House, also a Georgian building, with an octagonal entrance hall. On the Berkshire border **Bridge House** by the bridge on the Hungerford Road is seventeenth century with additions in 1766. On a knoll, in Berkshire, Chilton Lodge gazes over the valley.

Littlecote House is one of the great houses of Wiltshire and has recently changed its ownership for the fourth time in its long history. It is a brick built Tudor mansion although the oldest part is c. fifteenth century. In 1250 a house or hamlet of Littlecote stood hereabouts and before that a Romano-British villa was built in AD 170. Still to be seen in the grounds of Littlecote are the excavated remains of a Roman villa with its superb 'Orpheus' mosaic which was laid in AD 360.

Until the end of 1990 Littlecote was an outstanding tourist attraction. Recently bought by Peter de Savary amid much publicity it had undergone rapid changes and was once again a working estate with animals, craftsmen, falconry displays and jousting. The part of the house open to the public contained splendid oak furnishings, a ghost and a Cromwellian chapel. The experience provided a good sense of history. With its steam railway, woodland adventure playground, horse-drawn wagon tours and splendid grounds it really was a 'day out for all the family'.

With virtually no warning, and much to the dismay of tourists who are banging on the gate, the owner closed the entire operation apparently preferring a country house and golf course image. However, at the time of going to press I understand the recession has interfered with his plans.

Return south to Froxfield and the A4 and so back to Marlborough.

Dovecote, Avebury

VILLAGES OF THE ROYAL FORESTS

The dominating feature of Wiltshire, the chalk downs, includes not only Salisbury Plain, but also the area east of Marlborough where Savernake Forest was in existence before the Norman invasion. William the Conqueror gave the position of Hereditary Warden of the forest to one of his knights at the Battle of Hastings, Richard Esturmy. The Marquis of Ailesbury, whose family descended from the Esturmys, is the twenty-ninth Hereditary Warden to care for the forest, and he has written an interesting book called *A History of Savernake Forest*.

At one time the woodlands were overgrown and unkempt, a mixture of trees, thickets and undergrowth but still a favourite with the kings of England, who hunted here for the red and fallow deer with which the forest was stocked. It was not until the eighteenth century that the forest was taken in hand by that great landscaper, Launcelot 'Capability' Brown. At the time ownership had passed to the first Marquis of Ailesbury, Lord Bruce, who built Tottenham House, a mansion which still stands, though much enlarged, within the forest; it is now a school. Lord Bruce was married to the daughter of Henry Hoare (*see* Tour 18), creator of Stourhead, and while visiting Tottenham House, Henry Hoare encountered Capability Brown, who felt the unkempt forest had great capabilities'. (His vocabulary was liberally sprinkled with this word, hence his nickname.) It conjures up a fascinating picture of these two great men, riding or driving through the forest together, discussing a possible layout for the future Savernake Forest. Happily Lord Bruce accepted the proposals put to him, and he set about the mammoth task of beautifying and enclosing the forest, also laying out the Grand Avenue, suggested by Capability Brown, which is four miles long with eight roads meeting at its centre. In 1939 the Forestry Commission signed a 999-year tenancy agreement for the 'sylvicultural rights of Savernake', leaving the hereditary wardenship to the Marquess and his heirs. The forest today is wonderfully cared for, and the public has free access to its 4,000 cres of rides and walks (*see* TIC).

The Royal Forest of Chute extended from the neighbourhood of Savernake as far as Hampshire. It too was stocked with red deer, many of which ended up on the royal table or were sent to royal favourites. As with so many of our ancient woodlands, only pockets of forest remain. Extensive views over the woods and combes of this lovely part of Wiltshire can be seen from Chute Causeway, a road built in a great curve along a ridge of the downs. It is part of a Roman road from Old Sarum to Mildenhall and beyond, and is an unusual deviation from their normally straight routes. In this area, in 1927, a boy picked up and threw a globular flint. It broke open and its hollowed interior was found to contain 65 British gold coins, 29 of which were deposited in the British Museum; the rest are in the museum at Devizes. The boy received £50 from the Treasury.

The Royal Forests were much more extensive than they are today, and many of the villages described below stood within the forest. Occasionally a church spire and smoke from a chimney can be seen rising from the trees where a village is still hidden in its woodland setting.

Tour 11: Savernake and Chute

From Marlborough take the A4 to Froxfield and turn right opposite the Somerset Hospital, a building founded by Sarah, Duchess of Somerset in 1694 for 30 widows. The road over the canal leads to Little Bedwyn. At the crossroads turn right for Chisbury or left for Little Bedwyn. **Chisbury** was an Iron Age hill fort, and standing within its 50 foot high ramparts is the ruined chapel of St Martin's, now used as a farm building, with windows still bearing its thirteenth century tracery.

Little Bedwyn has a Norman church with an enormous yew tree and a magnificent spire. It is found at the end of a lane of Victorian houses. Across the railway and canal is the pedimented Georgian Manor Farmhouse. Close to the house is an octagonal former game larder, and on the other side a summer house which still has its eighteenth century plasterwork. There are some interesting farm buildings on the other side of the road.

Return to the crossroads and drive to **Great Bedwyn**, a village

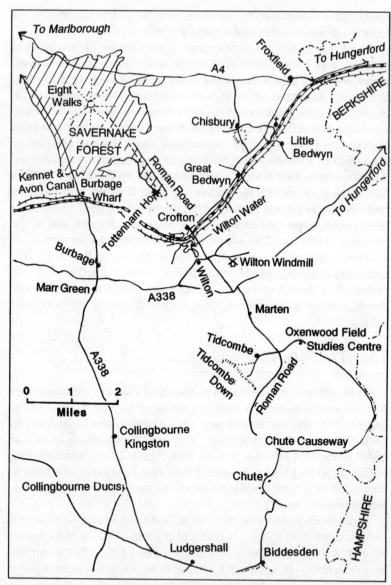

Tour 11: Savernake and Chute

once larger and more important than it is today. There is a tradition of stone masonry, and the **Stone Museum** (open daily) with monuments dating back to the eighteenth century can be visited by the public. A mile or two west of Great Bedwyn is **Crofton Pumping Station** (*see* TIC). It stands 400 feet above the source of the river Kennet at the summit of the Kennet and Avon Canal. In the nineteenth century two early Cornish beam engines – an 1812 Boulton and Watt and an 1845 Harvey's of Hayle – were installed to pump water to these upper reaches. Recently these massive engines have been restored by the Kennet and Avon Canal Trust, and may be visited by the public. Several times a year the beam engines are 'in steam', and at that time trips on the narrow boat *Jubilee* are available from Crofton Top Lock.

Farm building, Little Bedwyn

Backtrack from Crofton to the next right turn to **Wilton** (not to be confused with the town near Salisbury). It is a charming village with a duck pond fed by streams which wind through the gardens. A footpath near the pond takes the walker to Crofton Pumping Station by way of Wilton Water, a much larger pond which rises from a natural spring and is a feeder for the canal. (If you are at Crofton, perhaps walking to Wilton would be the best way to approach the village.)

On the way to Wilton by road, an unusual landmark on the hill is Wiltshire's only complete surviving windmill. Wilton Windmill was built in brick in 1821, and was worked until the 1890s. It fell into disuse, and was in a dilapidated condition when work started on its restoration in 1971. It was re-opened in 1979 and is now in full working order; it sells flour throughout the summer, when it is open to the public (usually on Sunday afternoons and bank holidays; *see* TIC). Just before Wilton village turn left towards **Tidcombe**. Cross the A338 for Marten and Tidcombe. The road to the latter is a right turn for a glimpse of this farming community with its flint and rubble church and large Manor House. It sits below Tidcombe Down, a place of embankments and other earthworks. The track at the end of the village takes the walker up on the down.

Return to the road which here becomes Chute Causeway, part of the Roman road from Old Sarum to Mildenhall which forms a great arc around some of the most attractive scenery in Wiltshire, a place of combes and hills, farms and well-built fences set among the earthworks, barrows and tumuli of ancient man. The Roman road continues, but a right turn will take you to the three Chute villages set amongst what is left of Chute Forest. The tiny villages with their churches, one of which is derelict, are worth discovering. **Lower Chute** has some fine buildings near a green, and around the corner is a charming old thatched pub called The Hatchet. Just before the pub, the road to Biddesden runs through the woods where, on the Hampshire border, Biddesden House stands imposingly at the end of a long drive. Architecturally important, it was built in 1711-12 for General Webb by an unknown architect. It is a huge brick building, seven bays by seven bays, and much attention has been paid to the symmetry of the façades. But this is broken on the north-east corner by an extraordinary castellated turret, said to have been built to house a bell brought home from Lille by the general. Long live eccentrics!

From here the road leads to Ludgershall. Now a sprawling town and once a place of importance, it has the only remaining castle ruin in Wiltshire other than Wardour Castle. Return to Marlborough on the A346. The road passes through Collingbourne Ducis and Collingbourne Kingston, both forest villages in medieval times but, like

Burbage to the north, they now stand in a treeless part of Wiltshire. **Collingbourne Ducis** derives its name from having once belonged to the Duchy of Lancaster. The tombs of the great Seymour family are in the thirteenth century church, a building largely rebuilt in Victorian times. Nearby is Church Farmhouse which has a long barn, weatherboarded and thatched. At Burbage Wharf the road crosses the canal and shortly enters Savernake Forest, described at the turn of the century as follows: 'It is as though here Nature herself has raised up a rival to Stonehenge in a sanctuary at least as old and still perfect in beauty'. (Taken from *Highways and Byways in Wiltshire* by Edward Hutton).

Cottage near Savernake Forest

Tour 12: *The River Bourne and Clarendon*

The lengthy River Bourne begins its journey near Burbage, once a village within Savernake Forest, and flows southward to join the Avon east of Salisbury. For two thirds of its length, the river is a winterbourne, and in summer and early winter no water is found

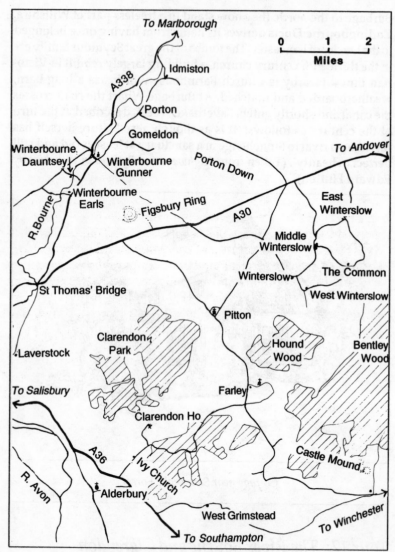

Tour 12: The River Bourne and Clarendon

north of Idmiston. At Idmiston, where watercress grows, the water forms a pond, then gathers momentum and increases in volume as it meanders down the valley towards Salisbury. Along its banks, going south, are the villages of Porton, Gomeldon and the Winterbournes – namely Gunner, Dauntsey and Earls.

This downland valley has seen continuous occupation since Stone Age and Bronze Age times, particularly around Winterslow where flint was mined from 1600 BC. There was much activity here in the Roman era, with roads radiating from Old Sarum, just north of Salisbury.

The great **Palace of Clarendon** in the royal forest of Clarendon began as a hunting lodge for Norman kings, and eventually became a place of retreat and pleasure to be visited by many of the great names in history. Thomas à Beckett lived in the thirteenth century in nearby Ford (itself a Roman river crossing for the Winchester road to Old Sarum). He was then a parish priest and used to walk to Clarendon Palace at the King's bidding to officiate at the services. After the Wars of the Roses, the Palace fell into disrepair, and when Queen Elizabeth I visited it when hunting in the forest, she found it almost uninhabitable.

Archaeologists started excavating in 1930 and continued intermittently until the war. They revealed Saxon evidence of a building below that of the Normans, and identified the main layout of the Palace rooms including the royal quarters, chapel and council chambers. It is sad that this royal residence, which played such a part in the political history of England, should now be reduced to a few fragments of stone buried in the woods as if it had never been.

The hills around the Bourne are now the home of the Chemical Defence and Microbiological Research Establishment. Because of the hush-hush nature of the work, large areas of Porton Down are closed to the public. This has had the effect of creating a huge nature reserve, and it is here that the Great Bustard, once a feature of the plains of Wiltshire and a delicacy at the king's table, has been repatriated. The bird appears on Wiltshire's coat of arms, and was the first bird to be protected by law. In the days of Henry VIII anyone taking a bustard egg was heavily fined.

Much of the area, especially around Tidworth, is covered with barracks, runways and army paraphernalia. But despite this invasion, life on the Plain goes on. Flora and fauna are much in evidence. Compromises have been reached between the farms and the army, and unemployment in the area has been considerably reduced.

For this tour, it is preferable to follow the river upstream, leaving Salisbury on the A30 going north. Where the road crosses the Bourne at St Thomas's Bridge, take the A338 to **Winterbourne Earls**. The church, which stands where the village merges with its neighbour **Winterbourne Dauntsey**, is Victorian and was built by T.H. Wyatt, who re-used materials from two local medieval churches that had been destroyed. The first house in the neighbouring village is an eighteenth century house called The Elms, with giant pilasters and five bays with round-arched windows. Also in Winterbourne Dauntsey is a Georgian manor house and The Grange, another eighteenth century house, both in brick with stone dressings.

Bourne Valley

At the junction with **Winterbourne Gunner** a minor road runs north on the right side of the river. Park near the corner of the minor road and walk along the main road to visit the church of St Mary, which is found by the river in a field at the end of a grassy path. It is made of flint and rubble, and has a squat Norman tower recently whitewashed and giving the church a continental appearance. The Early English south aisle has been demolished, but the arcade inside remains. South-west of the church is the white, railed tomb of Jane Tanner, who died in 1848 at a time when rural poverty was widespread and severe. Besides leaving one pound per annum for the maintenance of her tomb, she directed in her will that '30 families should receive five hundredweight of coal each, and flannel goods.' The very poor received one shilling a day. How grateful these villagers must have been at a time of great need.

Winterbourne Gunner takes its name from Gunnora, wife of Henry de la Mere who was lord of the manor at the time of Henry III. The road to the right near the junction allows access through the army camp and up to the downs beyond. It is an attractive road with good views, and where it joins the A30, the Iron Age hill fort called Figsbury Ring can be seen on the right. A track leads from the A30 to the hill fort, providing panoramic views.

Turn left on to the A30 and drive east for a couple of miles, looking for the Pheasant Hotel. Known until recent years as Winterslow Hut, it has associations with the essayist William Hazlitt who spent some time in **Winterslow** where his wife owned a cottage. Later, when he had separated from his wife, he resided at Winterslow Hut, where he wrote the *Winterslow Essays*. He was visited there occasionally by his friends Charles and Mary Lamb. In October 1816 Hazlitt witnessed an unusual incident: a travelling menagerie arrived at the inn, and a lioness escaped and attacked one of the leading horses of the Exeter mail. The lioness was eventually captured after great bravery shown by its keepers.

The scattered parish of Winterslow consists of East, West and Middle Winterslow, the last known locally as The Common. It takes its name from the Old English *wunters hloew* - burial mound. The ancient manor belonged to John de Roches at the time of the early Plantagenets, and his tenure involved a strange custom of making a 'pitcher of claret' whenever the King was at Clarendon Palace. Sir Benjamin Brodie, the famous surgeon, was born here in 1783 in a house which eventually burnt down, nearly killing a baby who later in life became Lord Holland, a notable Whig peer and patron of literature.

The name of Holland is closely connected with Winterslow. The Earls of Holland had estates in the area, and in the eighteenth century two attempts were made to build a grand country mansion, but both houses were burnt down, the second time during a ball to celebrate the completion of the mansion. Not surprisingly, they gave up, and instead built a new Holland House on their London estate, which included Mayfair and much of the West End. Many London names, such as Soho and Piccadilly, are found in the Winterslow area. The villages are high on the downs, and to the south the old Forest of Clarendon stretches as far as the border with Hampshire.

To the west lies the village of **Pitton**. Ralph Whitlock, writer and authority on his native county, resided here, and was born in the village. The little flint church has a Norman doorway and a thirteenth century porch with an interior that was restored by the Victorians. Besides some pretty cottages, the main attraction in Pitton is the Silver Plough, a pub which attracts people as far away as Salisbury to sample its exceptional menu.

Continue south from the Silver Plough to **Farley**. The village is on a loop and is known for its classical church, founded by Sir Stephen Fox who was a friend and contemporary of Sir Christopher Wren. The builder was Alexander Fort, master joiner of the Office of Works. This surprising building stands opposite the Fox Almshouses of 1681, ten years before the completion of the church. Fox, who was born in Farley of lowly parentage, somehow inveigled his way into the court of Charles I. He later became Paymaster-General of the Forces, and the considerable fortune he accumulated gave him ideas of grand estates. However his son did not live up to his father's expectation of being heir to a dynasty, so late in life Fox married again, and much to his delight his wife produced twins. One became the first Ear of Holland (see above) and the other the first Earl of Ilchester.

From Farley pass through East Grimstead on the way to West Dean a few miles to the east. **West Dean** is a pretty village with a station, a motte-and-bailey castle mound and houses which straddle the Wiltshire/Hampshire border. It was the home of the Evelyn family, who produced the famous diarist John Eveyln. The tiny chantry chapel, which was attached to the now demolished church of St Mary, was preserved, and with it a fine collection of memorials to the Evelyns and the Pierrepoints, including a remarkable tomb with doors of wood which open to reveal a life-size statue of Robert Pierrepoint, Earl of Kingston, who married a daughter of the Evelyns. The chapel was built by Robert de Borback in 1333, and stands in the trees on the top of a hill. Nearby the castle mound with a dry moat tells of a more remote past. More ancient still are the remains of three Roman villas found in the area.

Return to the A36 through West Grimstead and turn right at Whaddon, passing through Alderbury (described in Tour 14). On the outskirts of Salisbury, a road to the right goes through **Laverstock**. Here the Bourne makes an attractive picture as it runs through gardens and under the bridge before joining the Avon just south of the main road.

VILLAGES NORTH AND SOUTH OF SALISBURY

The Avon valley between Amesbury and Salisbury, with its proximity to Stonehenge, Ogbury Camp and Old Sarum, must have prehistoric associations of which we know nothing. It is surprising that this stretch of river valley with its fertile meadows and great beauty has not seen more development such as is found along the banks of the Upper Avon north of Amesbury, where housing and military establishments have mushroomed since the 1950s. In part this must be due to the landowners and farmers resisting change, and may this always be so; for here is one of the most idyllic and unspoilt valleys in Wiltshire, where thatched cottages, manor houses and ancient churches blend perfectly with their riverside setting.

Tour 13: The Avon north of Salisbury

Just south of the major road which rushes the visitor to Stonehenge is the small community of **West Amesbury**. Here a charming row of red brick cottages with flint decoration and topped with thick thatching stands near West Amesbury House, a flint-and-stone building of the seventeenth century. Behind the façade of the house can be seen the remains of a medieval building, and still visible are an ancient wooden screen, two arched doorways, and in the west wing, the medieval roof. Beyond the cottages is a house with a sign called The Fighting Cocks, with woven cockerels perched on the thatched roof where no doubt dubious entertainment once took place. The river meanders on down the valley past **Wilsford**, with the squat Norman tower of its church standing among the trees, and Wilsford House, a neo-Jacobean building designed by Detmar Blow in 1905. This architect must have had a special affinity for this valley, for further on is **Lake House** (garden open for NGS and GS; *see* Gardens Open), a sixteenth century flint-and-stone mansion built by

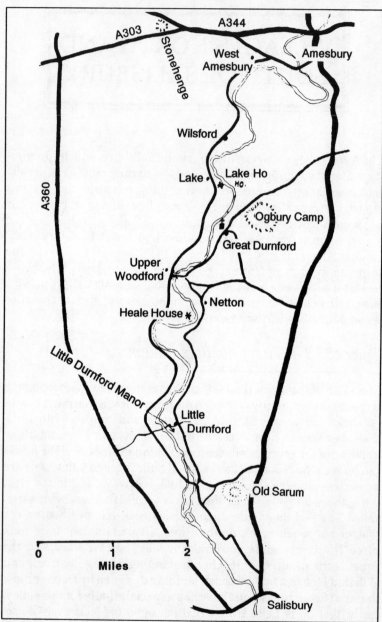

Tour 13: The Avon north of Salisbury

a wealthy clothier, George Duke. It was beautifully restored by Detmar Blow in 1898 before it was gutted by fire in 1912 and again rebuilt. Detmar Blow was also responsible for the enlargement of Heale House (garden open for NGS and GS; see Gardens Open), a few miles south, near Woodford; and again in 1900 he built the last cottage on the Salisbury Road at Netton.

The village of **Lake** is particularly pretty, having a mill and thatched cottages standing close to the river, and the splendidly imposing Lake House mentioned above with its turrets, castellations and topiary in the forecourt. Further south, just before entering **Upper Woodford**, is a large farmhouse with a most unusual outbuilding with a neo-Georgian clock turret. This eye-catching object was erected in 1935 to commemorate George V's Silver Jubilee: the designer was Darcy Braddell, who undertook the rebuilding of Lake House after the fire.

The bridge at Upper Woodford is the only crossing place for traffic along this stretch of the river. On the east bank lies Great

The Avon at Great Durnford

Durnford. Cross the bridge and take the first turn left. **Great Durnford** is a most attractive village with great and small houses and much thatching. The road ends with a private drive to a red-brick manor house set beautifully on the banks of the Avon and which is now a school. At the entrance to the drive the road swings round to the right and winds up to Ogbury Camp, an Iron Age hill fort of 62 acres much of which is now under the plough.

Of all the churches in the valley, St Andrew's in Great Durnford is surely the finest. Ancient wall paintings adorn its leaning walls;

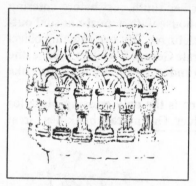

Norman font,
Great Durnford Church

odd, lozenge-flower carvings climb in a vertical, unfinished band up the inside of the north door. One Norman south window can be seen inside but it is blocked, and outside it is hidden by a Norman buttress. The north and south doors have interesting carving and tympana containing squares of green and white stone. The north doorway has a band of what look like shuttlecocks, six of which are well preserved, and both doors have bands of zig-zags. The carved Norman chancel arch leads to the chancel, built in about 1200 with lancet windows. The font is a remarkable Norman piece with interlacing arches, while the rough pews behind the font date back to the fourteenth century.

Just south of the Black Horse Inn, a footpath leads over the meadow to the mill. Here it is possible to cross the swirling waters of the river by way of ancient wooden footbridges. The footpath continues downstream to the road bridge. Near the mill, where weeping willows dip into the water, St Andrew's Church can be seen in the distance across the meadows.

Over the centuries the population of the valley has not altered a great deal. The chief occupation has always been farming, although this has been considerably reduced in recent times through mechanization. It seems that the river has provided employment in various ways, and was economically important. Water meadows were made in the seventeenth century, and withy beds form part of manor surveys. Weaving did not become a cottage industry, as it had done in so many other places, until just before 1900, when a spinning industry was started in Lake at Lake House, and employed and trained local women. However, this developed into the Stonehenge Woollen Industry of Amesbury, and is no longer connected with the valley.

The booklet *The Woodford Valley: a History of its Churches, People and Places*, which can be bought in St Andrew's church, makes interesting reading while visiting this lovely valley. Besides details of buildings, occupations and historical changes, it brings the long dead people of the area to life in a fascinating section on the wills of ordinary people, and gives us a glimpse into their characters, emotions and concern for their families.

The Iron Age fort and site of **Old Sarum** (open daily) are of immense historical interest, and are found one-and-a-half miles north of Salisbury. If you drive south from Durnford, you will see signs to it. The remains of this massive 28-acre hill fort are evident, but the great amount of activity that went on inside its boundaries in later centuries has all but disappeared. Little excavation has been done on the defences of the Iron Age fort, as they are masked by Norman additions, but some Roman and pre-Roman material suggest that it was occupied in the earlier Iron Age period and also in the first and third centuries AD. Four Roman roads meet outside the fort, which indicates its importance at that time. In Saxon times it seems a major battle was fought in 552, in which the Saxons put the Britons to flight. When the Normans arrived, they realised its potential as a defensive town, and set about building, not only a castle, but a town and a cathedral. The outlines of the buildings and some walls remain, but except for the castle, Old Sarum was abandoned in the thirteenth century.

Although they are not described here in detail, the villages of the Upper Avon are of beauty and interest. South of **Upavon**, the minor roads which link the villages on the east side of the river are particularly attractive, and take the visitor to **Enford, Fittleton, Netheravon** (with its part-Saxon Church) and **Durrington**, all of which have grown up close to the river with a backdrop of woodland. While these villages are being enjoyed, a visit to **Stonehenge** (open daily) or nearby **Woodhenge** (open daily) might be included in the itinerary.

Tour 14: The Avon south of Salisbury

To the south of Salisbury the Avon flows across wide open meadows and disappears into Hampshire at Downton. This south-east corner of Wiltshire points towards Southampton and the coast, but approaching from the north, the visitor will be unaware of the large conurbations to the south. This part of Wiltshire has small and large villages of interest and beauty, although many of the residents find work in the larger places of Salisbury, Romsey and Southampton. Here the New Forest merges with the hills of the chalklands, and from **Pepperbox Hill** just off the A36, unsurpassed views of the Hampshire Basin are included in the panorama.

A mile or two south of Salisbury on the A338 is the turn to Britford. Both Britford and nearby Longford are, as their names suggest, old fording places and important crossings in their day as bridges were few.

Britford is a peaceful village in a rural setting with lovely views of Salisbury Cathedral across the meadows. Of particular note are Bridge Farm, a large eighteenth century house near the river, and The Moat, a splendid part-Georgian and part-nineteenth century Gothic house with castellated bays and ogee-headed windows with a moat around and about it. At the end of the lane past The Moat is the church of St John's, begun in Saxon times. It is surprisingly large, cruciform in shape, and with a tower which was renewed in 1767. The crossing arches beneath the tower are fourteenth century, and the chancel east window has tracery of the Decorated Period. The tall nave with its high windows, the south doorway and the two arches at the end of the nave are all Saxon. Running up the north doorway and around the arch is some exquisite Saxon moulding – a carving of scrolls enclosing bunches of grapes and also some complicated interlacing patterns executed with great delicacy by a Saxon craftsman. The south arch has been left undecorated except for the insertion of some Roman tiles. The chancel has an impressive altar tomb under a carved arch, and was brought here in the eighteenth century with no record of to whom it belonged. An ancient stone altar lies under the present one. The church register includes a story of two women who are buried in the churchyard. In 1653 one of the women boxed the other on her ear, from which blow she subsequently died; the other was hanged for her deed at Salisbury Fair.

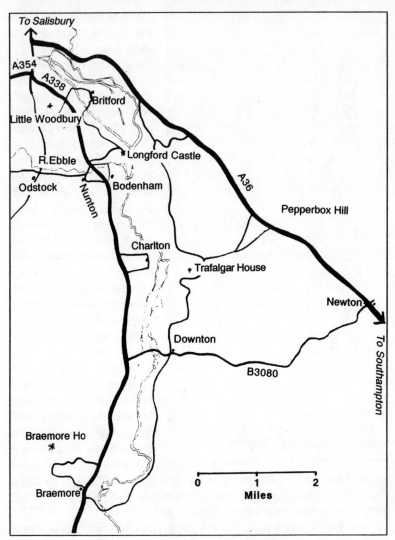

Tour 14: The Avon south of Salisbury

Saxon moulding, Britford church

Near Britford is one of the most famous of Wiltshire's great houses – Longford Castle. It stands in a park of 250 acres on the banks of the Avon, and was built between 1575 and 1591 by Sir Thomas Gorges, whose tomb can be found in the cathedral. It is a strange, triangular house of patterned flint and stone, squat round towers, many chimneys, small domes and finials. Before the building was finished, Sir Thomas ran out of money, but his wife, a former lady-in-waiting to Queen Elizabeth I, was determined it should be completed. When a ship from the Armada ran aground on coastal land belonging to Sir Thomas, his wife begged the hull from the Queen, who granted the wish – not knowing that it contained much treasure, which was used to finish the building. Longford Castle houses a unique collection of furniture and paintings, but is a private residence and not open to the public.

South of Britford, just off the A338, is **Charlton**, which has a farm and a barn set on staddles at its entrance. It is a charming village of thatched and timbered cottages, with the river running close by. Standing on a bluff the other side of the river and approached from Alderbury is Trafalgar House, built in 1733 and at that time known as Standlynch House. In 1814 it was given by the nation to Nelson's heirs, hence its present name. Many architects had a hand in its building, including John Wood the Younger, who added the wings, and Nicholas Revett who designed the elaborate porch with 14 Doric columns.

Close to the Hampshire border and situated on either side of the Avon on the B3080 is **Downton**, and being an ancient borough is by definition 'an inhabited place larger than a village', but it has a village appearance, especially the central part known as The Borough, with its timbered and thatched cottages, White Horse Inn and remains of the Borough Cross. Towards the river The Borough narrows before it crosses the Avon by way of three bridges to join the High Street, which in turn winds up to the historic mound known as The Moot. This was the site of a Norman castle of the Bishops of Winchester, but is now topped by a fine seventeenth century house called Moot House, which took advantage of the site by creating a garden in and around the earthwork. To the south is the church of St Lawrence, dating also from Norman times and having a nave with circular piers and scalloped capitals, although the pointed arches are of a more Transitional nature. The transepts with their lancet windows are Early English, and there are traces of the Decorated period in the chancel. In the eighteenth century height was added to the nave using a red and purple brick which gives it a rather odd appearance. There is a wealth of Georgian monuments mainly to the Feversham family, and the interior is impressive in its spaciousness and airiness. Nearby is The Tannery, which tends to dominate the scene and which is still in production today. In recent years Downton has revived an old festival known as the Cuckoo Fair, which had its origins in the 1600s to welcome the first cuckoo of spring.

The B3080 merges with a minor road at **Redlynch** (Jacobean house open to the public – New House, Redlynch; *see* TIC) which turns east to join the A36 at Newton. Two miles to the north is the turning to Pepperbox Hill. The shape of Eyre's Folly on the hill gives Pepperbox its name. It was built in 1606 by Giles Eyre, who was envious of the towers of nearby Longford Castle. He built his octagonal folly in brick with bands of brick for decoration. The 70 acres of downland and woods are owned by the National Trust, and on a clear day the views stretch to the Isle of Wight.

The main road back to Salisbury passes through **Alderbury**, once a royal forest village and an important place in the heyday of Clarendon Palace (*see* Tour 12). Parts of it are still wooded and it stands above the Avon with a view of Salisbury's spire across the stream-strewn meadows. On the other side of the river is Longford

Castle (*see* above). The Victorian church built by S.S.Teulon in 1858 has an attractive broach spire on a gabled tower. Nearby is Alderbury House which is said to have material from the Cathedral's demolished campanile in its walls. North of the main road is Ivychurch, the site of an Augustinian Priory founded by Henry II and demolished in 1888.

View across the meadows to Salisbury

Half a mile to the north is Clarendon House, not to be confused with the long demolished Clarendon Palace. It is a privately owned, large, classical mansion built in 1737 standing amid fine parkland and has a dovecote with a cupola and clock. The strange house called St Marie's Grange, which is found north-west of the village on the main road, was built in 1835 by Pugin for himself and his new wife when he was only 23. He must have enjoyed building his dream house but stayed in it only two years before going to London to work on the new Houses of Parliament. Alderbury has two inns, one of which is the Three Crowns which has royal connotations; the other is the Green Dragon which was 'The Blue Dragon' in Dickens' *Martin Chuzzlewit*.

VILLAGES WEST
OF SALISBURY

Between the Nadder and the Ebble valleys rise the rampart hills of chalk which give the Ebble its other name of Chalkebourne. To the south lie the ridges of Cranborne Chase rich in prehistoric earthworks and renowned for their beauty and spectacular views. An ancient Ridgeway crosses the hills high above the river, and another Roman road on a straight course from Old Sarum points to the southwest, crossing the Ebble at Stratford Tony. In medieval times the population may have been greater than today. Much of the land belonged to the abbesses of Wilton and Shaftesbury, but after the Dissolution, passed to the earls of Pembroke to whom much of the land still belongs. With the massive hill barrier to the north the history of the Ebble valley is connected more with Cranborne Chase. Many of the large imposing houses, particularly in Broad Chalke, were erected by farmers from the Chase who descended to the valley in winter. These in turn have become the homes of admirals, generals and brigadiers who have found one of the most charming, peaceful and unspoilt places in the south of England in which to write their memoirs and tend their gardens.

Tour 15: *Villages of the Ebble*

Although the villages are like beads along a string it is the string that has the greatest appeal. The little river rises near Alvediston and runs only some 13 miles before emptying into the Avon south of Salisbury. Although full of life in winter it is little more than a stream, but a stream which is much used and loved. Watercress beds abound, particularly at Broad Chalke where the volume of the water increases with the addition of the stream from Bowerchalk. Here the road crosses the beds showing the interesting system of irrigation. Wherever possible gardens surround or run close by the stream providing

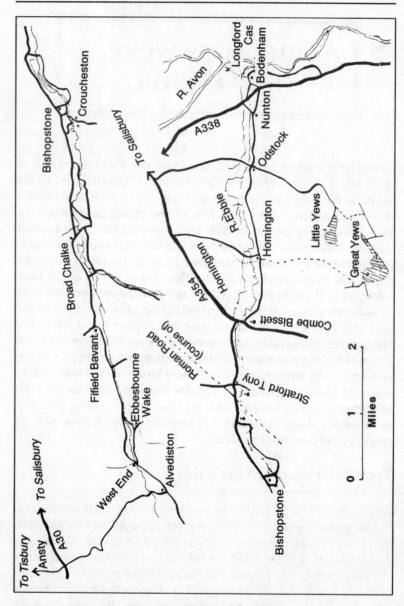

Tour 15: Villages of the Ebble

excuses for little stone bridges and the perfection of an English garden landscape.

For some reason it is important to follow a river downstream rather than upstream. Driving west from Salisbury the A30 passes through Wilton and in about 10 miles a sign to the left points to **Alvediston** (Ansty to the right). The road crosses the great chalk mass of Swallowcliffe Down and there is an exhilarating hairpin bend half way up the hill. If one was walking instead of driving the local name of 'Ellofadistance' for the village of Alvediston would be very apt!

The church of St Mary is at the north end of the village and looks south across the meadows. The church was rebuilt by T.H.Wyatt, although the Perpendicular tower remains. The effigy of a knight in armour is that of Sir John Gawen whose family held the manor of Alvediston in medieval times. The name is thought to link with the Gawain who was one of King Arthur's knights. The Wyndhams, who are also commemorated in the church, bought Norrington Manor from the Gawen family. The part medieval, part Elizabethan house lies about a mile from the village in the hills.

Turn left at the T-junction towards Ebbesbourne Wake. At West End the road divides. Take the lower road where the river gushes under little bridges before flowing through the meadows towards **Fifield Bavant**. Here the little church on the hill has one thirteenth

Fifield Bavant

century lancet window and a Norman font, and its only approach is through the farmyard. Pevsner wonders if it is the smallest parish church in Wiltshire.

Broad Chalke is the largest village in the valley. The first road to the right spans the watercress beds and it is interesting to see how the river has been used for the purpose. Remain on the south side of the river and continue through the village. There are some fine houses which were the winter residences of the wealthy Cranborne Chase farmers. The small eighteenth century brick manor house called Reddish Manor is particularly noteworthy as is the Old Rectory west of the church. The large cruciform church dates from the late thirteenth century, its simple wagon roof also probably dating from that time. The tower sits on a vaulted crossing and the transepts have lancet windows, the north window being unusually fine. John Aubrey lived for a while at Broad Chalke and became church-warden. Along the road to the east, before recrossing the river, is Knighton Manor with a sixteenth century doorway.

There is another large cruciform church at **Bishopstone**. It dates from Norman times but is mainly of the Decorated period with elaborate mouldings and much detail. The chancel and south transept are wonderfully ornate and are crowned by rib-vaulting. It is a splendid church. Watercress beds are again much in evidence and at Croucheston the mill makes further use of the river. Two seventeenth century buildings, Netton Farmhouse and Faulstone House, are of flint and stone; Bishopstone House, built in 1815, is of grey brick and Throope Manor to the east of the village dates from Georgian times.

'Strete-ford', a crossing of the Roman road, gives **Stratford Tony** its prefix. Ralph Toni was William the Conqueror's standard bearer at the Battle of Hastings and was rewarded with land here. The church dates from the thirteenth century but is mainly Decorated.

At **Coombe Bissett** the road crosses the A354. At the junction turn right over the bridge and left before the church. There is much to see at this crossroads. The seventeenth century bridge replaces the old packhorse bridge found a little way downstream. The large church, with its Norman south door and Norman arcade, sits on a grassy knoll opposite the river where a pool and a picturesque barn attract the ducks.

The river continues to run nearby as the road passes through **Homington**. Here the road divides and it is worth taking the left fork through the village if only to see the newly thatched walls of an imposing entrance. To the left of this property a footpath takes the walker over the river to Homington Down. From the valley road a track on the right leads to the downs to the south and to the ancient groves and avenues of two yew woods known as Great and Little Yews. One side of Great Yews forms the boundary of Grim's Ditch and has prehistoric origins. Seven avenues of yews meet in the centre of the wood.

The valley road continues to Odstock. Here the attractive flint and chequerwork church is never locked because of a gipsy curse from long ago. *The Odstock Curse* was the title of a radio play by Ralph Whitlock and this dramatic tale is set out in detail in his book *The Folklore of Wiltshire*.

A short distance from the A338 lies **Nunton** with its largely Victorian church by T.H.Wyatt. Nunton House, east of the church, is an early eighteenth century mansion which opens its garden gates to the public through the National Gardens Scheme (*see* Gardens Open). The house faces south overlooking the garden and was supposedly built by a rich merchant from Salisbury who fell in love with a girl from a nearby farm. She would only marry him if the house he built was within sight of her mother's. This he did but made sure that it faced the other way!

Bodenham, on the east side of the A338, is one of the entrances to Longford Park. Past the thatch and timbered houses a pretty lane leads to a wide stretch of the Avon where it has its confluence with the Ebble.

Tour 16: Villages of the Nadder

Although the Nadder Valley is fairly well populated, the small villages are often found away from the river, situated on tributaries which run into the Nadder. This is an area where local stone has been used extensively in the buildings, and much good stone has come from the Portland and Purbeck beds near Tisbury. The stone which went into the building of Salisbury Cathedral and Wilton house is the famous Chilmark stone which geologically belongs to the Portland beds. These beds are part of the band of stone known as Jurassic Oolitic limestone which runs throughout the country from Yorkshire to Dorset.

This lush valley, often incised by combes with thickly wooded

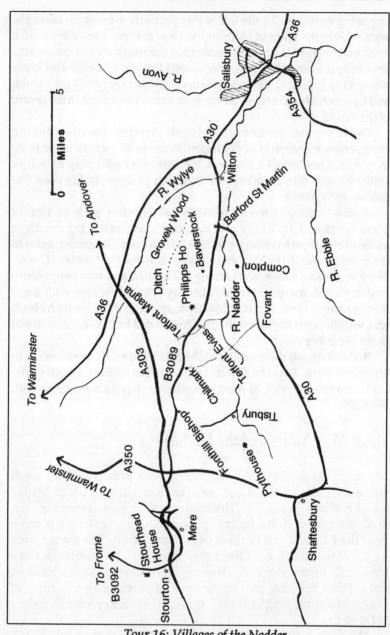

Tour 16: Villages of the Nadder

sides, has the advantage of a Greensand ridge, a sedimentary out-crop of sandstone, which not only produces a greenish-grey building stone but gives rise to a very fertile soil. Here in the Nadder Valley fruit growing used to be abundant in the eighteenth and nineteenth centuries, particularly around Dinton. Watercress was also grown extensively where the streams were dammed to form large ponds, one or two of which are now being adapted for fish farming.

From Salisbury take the A30 to Wilton then the B3089 through the valley at **Barford St Martin**, where the road crosses the river. Here at the crossroads are some pleasant houses including the eighteenth century Green Dragon Inn. The church is mainly thirteenth century, and nearby is part of the ancient village cross. On the downs to the north is a large Iron Age settlement, part of which is within Grovely Wood.

The river runs near the little hamlet of **Baverstock** before the road leaves its banks. **Dinton** is found north of the river, its northern boundary being the great Grovely Grim's Dyke. This great earth-work comprising a low bank with a ditch on the north side almost certainly dates from the Iron Age and runs along the ridge from Grovely Hill westwards for almost nine miles. The Nadder is the southern boundary of the parish, and here in the seventeenth century the floating water meadow became popular, providing fertile land for the growing of fodder for dairy cattle by way of irrigation channels, traces of which can be seen today. In 1962 meadows were again being flooded in this way.

The old part of the village of Dinton is found on the road which runs north past the church. Many buildings are noteworthy. In a small village it is surprising to find that the National Trust owns no less than four houses, including the imposing mansion called **Philipps House** (*see* TIC) earlier known as Dinton House and before that, Dinton Park. In 1689 George Smith sold his estate to Richard Wyndham. The Wyndham family lived in the old house until it was replaced in the early nineteenth century. The architect was Sir Jeffrey Wyatt (later known as Wyattville) and the house, built of Chilmark stone, was probably based on his design for **Pyt House** (*see* TIC) near Tisbury, seven miles away (*see* Tour 17). It stands at the top of its extensive grounds with a backdrop of trees, a classical building of fine proportions, having a large portico with Ionic columns support-ing the pediment. The interior has a splendid staircase lit by a dome in the roof. Philipps House is used at present as a conference centre for the YWCA, and can be visited by the public by written appointment.

The other National Trust houses are not open to the public. The first is Lawes Cottage, the home of William Lawes, the seventeenth century composer. East of Lawes Cottage is Little Clarendon (visits by prior written appointment only), with a gabled two-storey porch. Hyde's House, north-west of the church, is the birthplace of Edward Hyde, first earl of Clarendon. The church is mainly from the Decorated period, although it dates from the thirteenth century and has an impressive group of tower arches and a fine west window in the nave – a good example of the Decorated style.

Teffont Magna and its neighbour **Teffont Evias** are picturebook villages of great charm. Teffont Magna, which for centuries was a chapelry of the parish of Dinton, was joined to Teffont Evias in 1934 to form the parish of Teffont. The most northerly part of the ancient parish lay 600 feet up on the chalk downs before descending 300 feet to the foothills, only to rise again on a ridge of Upper Greensand which borders the chalk. At Springhead a stream, the Teff, emerges from the chalk and channels its way through the Greensand to gurgle merrily through the village, passing under many little stone bridges to fill the lake in the meadow beyond the Manor, before joining the Nadder. The parish boundary stops half-a-mile short of the river, and did not therefore have the benefit of the fertile valley which Dinton exploited in the nineteenth century. The chalklands of the ancient parish were devoted to sheep and corn, and it was not until this century that fertilizers provided a richer soil to allow mixed farming in the area.

The two villages with their little bridges leading to seventeenth and eighteenth century cottages, the two churches (one thirteenth and one nineteenth century) and the old Black Horse Inn found between the two provides a setting of pure English beauty and tranquillity. Among the cottages are some larger houses, one of which is Fitz House (see NGS), which was a farmhouse till the 1920s. The late sixteenth century or early seventeenth century house has stone mullioned windows, and with an adjoining barn covers three sides of a square. The addition of a wing by R.Fitz in 1700 projects at the south end, and was originally a storehouse for wool. The gardens have recently been opened to the public for two days a week (*see* TIS). The Black Horse Inn also has mullioned windows, and is early eighteenth century. It is advisable to leave the car and walk through at least part if not both of the villages.

The church of St Michael and All Angels at Teffont Evias (or Ewyas) is linked with that of a church at Ewyas Harold in Herefordshire. The family of Ewyas owned land in Teffont in the thirteenth century. In the seventeenth century the name Evias (originally derived from the Welsh *ewig*, a ewe) was first used, and both spellings of the name are currently in use. The church with its lovely steeple had its origins in the twelfth century. It was virtually rebuilt in 1821 by John Mayne, the lord of the manor, and its setting with the Manor nearby is surely one of the most attractive groups of buildings in Wiltshire.

By contrast, the church in Teffont Magna is small and chapel-like, and dates also from the thirteenth century, although Saxon remains have been discovered. It too forms a delightful picture with the Teff running by and a group of thatched cottages on the corner.

The road near the Post Office leads to **Chilmark**. The first use of Chilmark stone was for roads constructed by the Romans to carry lead and silver from their mines in the Mendips to Winchester by way

Chilmark

of Old Sarum. The name is now linked with Salisbury and Winchester Cathedrals and many other buildings, including the village church of St Margaret of Antioch in Chilmark.

The church stands above the village, from where one sees a conglomeration of ancient roofs and stone houses. The church is generally of Early English appearance, and has a fine stone vaulted crossing beneath the tower, possibly built before 1300. The chancel has lancet windows typical of the Early English period, but the earliest part is a re-set doorway of *c*. 1200 which is now in the west wall of the north aisle. The tower holds a broach spire built in 1760. The Victorians did the rest of the interior, and overall it is a very pleasant building. The coffin table under the lych-gate is thought to be unique. The seventeenth century manor, south of the church, has mullioned windows and a little courtyard with a scrolled wall. Chilmark House is late Georgian and has a porch with green Doric columns. The Elizabethan rectory, set in parklike grounds, has a reputation for being haunted by a young woman, a tale which started in the early 1800s.

A minor road turns south at Chilmark and returns to the south bank of the Nadder before joining the A30. A mile or so east is **Compton Chamberlayne** and the thirteenth century church lying near Compton Park contains the vault of the Penruddockes who built the house in 1550 and lived there until this century. Sir John Penruddocke was executed in 1655 following efforts to establish Charles II as King in Salisbury. The magnificent house has an incomparable setting on the banks of the Nadder.

SOUTH-WEST WILTSHIRE

This area is within easy reach of Salisbury and Warminster and with its neighbouring county of Dorset provides some of the most beautiful scenery in Wiltshire from the heights of Cranborne Chase. The rivers Nadder and Ebble run almost parallel to each other on their way to join the Avon, and the valley villages are scattered over the lush meadows among leafy lanes. In the middle is one of two ancient castles left standing in Wiltshire and, like Ludgershall Castle, it is a ruin. **Old Wardour Castle** (*see* TIC) is one of the most spectacular ruins in southern England and stands near the new **Wardour Castle** (*see* TIC), both castles being the home of the earls of Arundel for nearly four centuries until 1944. Both castles may be visited.

Tour 17. Tisbury to Cranborne Chase

The impressive gateway at **Fonthill Bishop** stands at the entrance to the park of William Beckford's Gothic dream – Fonthill Abbey,. His dream was short-lived as his amazing mansion was destroyed by the collapse of its rather unstable but magnificent central tower. By then Beckford had lost the fortune that enabled him to build his home in 1790 and had gone to live in a more stable tower built for him on Lansdown Hill at Bath. His great legacy however comes to us by way of the trees he planted in the park which have reached splendid maturity. At the south end of the park is the Beckford Arms with a pleasant garden from where the spire of the Victorian church at **Fonthill Gifford** can be seen through the trees.

Driving east we find **Tisbury**, not quite a village, but rather one of Wiltshire's oldest small towns and included here because of its interesting church. At the bottom and to the right of the steep main street with its lovely old buildings, and close by the banks of the Nadder, stands St John the Baptist Church. It is a large cruciform

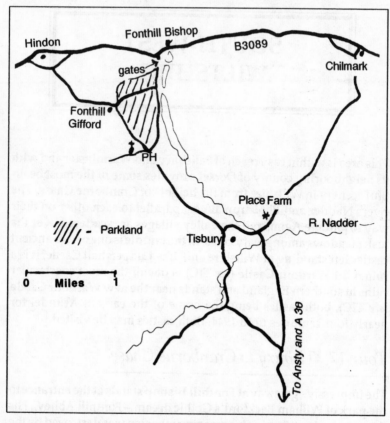

Tour 17: Tisbury to Cranbourne Chase

building of local Portland stone with a central tower, the upper part of which was replaced in 1762 after the spire collapsed. The oldest part of the building is the base of the tower which is carried on massive piers joined by pointed arches. This low narrow crossing is essentially Norman but the round arch has now given way to the pointed arch. This innovation took place towards the end of the twelfth century and by the early thirteenth century the rounded arch had disappeared. Tisbury is a good example of this transition time although the main body of the church is of the Decorated and Perpendicular periods. One of its glories is the wagon roof of the nave with horizontal angels attached to the hammerbeams.

In the churchyard look for an enormous yew tree with its base full

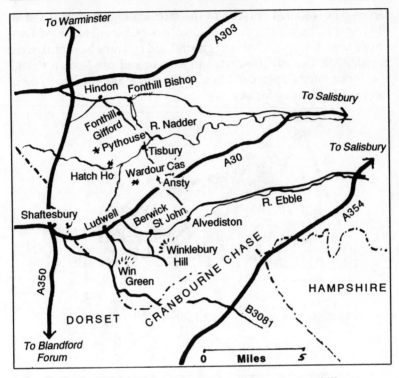

Tour 17: Detail of map opposite showing the Fonthills

of concrete but still going strong. Search also for the graves of Rudyard Kipling's parents. Wander out of the churchyard on the west side and stroll along the path beside the River Nadder.

Half a mile from the church along the river valley to the east of Tisbury is Place Farm with its enormous barn built in the fifteenth century. It is the largest barn in England, built of stone with 1,450 square yards of thatching and is part of a splendid group of buildings built in the fourteenth and fifteenth centuries as a monastic grange of Shaftesbury Abbey.

Drive south from Tisbury through the lanes and, in a wooded valley before climbing to the A30, is the pretty little village of **Ansty** with a duck pond, a very tall flagpole and an Early English church with a bellcote. At the junction with the A30 turn right and in three miles, on entering **Ludwell**, turn left. The old Roman road rises to join the B3081. Just before this junction a track to the left leads to **Win**

Green. The National Trust owns this outstanding viewpoint and at 910 feet it is the highest point of Cranborne Chase. The Chase was once a royal forest and hunting ground and this now beautiful open countryside, densely populated in Roman and pre-Roman times, was for centuries a place of forest rights and feuds and has its own long and fascinating history.

Tithe Barn, Place Farm, near Tisbury

From Win Green a track going east takes the walker along the ancient Ridgeway before it turns south and drops down to Tollard Royal, a distance of about three miles. Before descending the hill a minor road leads along the ridge to **Winklebury Hill**, a great Iron Age hill-fort, which rises steeply from the Ebble Valley below. At its foot is **Berwick St John** where, 200 years ago, a kindly rector left a legacy in his will for the church bell to be rung for 15 minutes at 8 o'clock every evening in winter to guide people down from the hills.

Tollard Royal can be approached either by foot, as described above, or by car on the B3081. The village is close to the Wiltshire / Dorset border and known for King John's Hunting Lodge and its one time owner and restorer, General Pitt-Rivers. The General won his rank in the Crimean War but found fame as a scientist and archaeologist. His house in London was filled with his collections which he presented to Oxford University in 1883. He had already moved to Tollard Royal and his house was known as Rushmore Lodge which is found in a clearing in the trees north of the village and is now Sandroyd School. His prehistory excavations began in earnest and he built up another fine collection which he housed in a museum built by him, at Farnham two miles away in Dorset. One of his most exciting finds was a Saxon cemetery containing 31 burials on Winklebury Hill. Details of his excavations are set out in five volumes. He also wrote a book on primitive locks and keys and one on Benin art.

For a while General Pitt-Rivers owned King John's House and opened it to the public. The centre of the house dates from c. 1240 with medieval additions and restoration of the sixteenth century. It is a delight to visit with its combined stone and wood construction providing a medieval atmosphere. The General laid out gardens here and also at Larmer Grounds 'for the recreation of the people in the neighbouring towns and villages. Everything he did was for the interest, education and pleasure of ordinary people. There is a memorial to the General and his wife in the partly rebuilt, thirteenth century church. They were born in the same year of 1810 and died within the same week in 1866. A great sadness was when their daughter was killed by lightning while on her honeymoon in Switzerland. The wooden cross in the church was made by Swiss peasants in memory of the girl who died.

Return on the B3081 across the high ridges of Cranborne Chase for the descent down Zigzag Hill to Shaftesbury in Dorset. From here, back in Wiltshire, the A350 leads north through lovely country, passing through the village of **East Knoyle**, the village where Sir Christopher Wren was born and where his father Dr Wren was appointed rector in 1623. Near 'Wren's Shop' on the main road is a memorial stone to the architect. Above the village is a house called 'Clouds' built in 1886 by Philip Webb for the Wyndhams at the cost of £80,000. After three years another £35,000 was spent on rebuilding it after a fire.

Three miles to the north on the B3089 is **Hindon**. It was founded by the Bishops of Winchester between 1220 and 1250 but due to a disastrous fire in 1754 there is very little of the original village left. Using Portland stone from the nearby Tisbury quarries Hindon was rebuilt. It has a wide attractive High Street and in the nineteenth century had 11 inns, as it became an important staging post for coaches between London and Exeter. Its decline came with the coming of the railways and the population dwindled. It has some fine houses attributable to its former affluence and is a pleasant place worthy of a visit.

Staddles near Hindon

Tour 18: Stourton and Stourhead

The village of **Stourton** in the south-west corner of the county, where Wiltshire, Dorset and Somerset meet, is the gateway to the mansion of **Stourhead** and its gardens of international fame. The village has a charm of its own consisting of the church of St Peter, the village inn, a row of eighteenth century cottages and one or two other attractive buildings. Beyond the village, although seemingly part of it, stands the Bristol High Cross. From the other side of the lake, cross and church form an exquisite picture, and were an integral part of Henry Hoare's vision for his wonderful landscape.

The church is the resting place of the Hoare family and the Stourtons who came before them. Built chiefly in the late medieval period, it has picturesque parapets of pierced triangles which were added at the time of Colt Hoare, the historian, in the eighteenth century. Inside, the arcades and chancel arch may be as early as the fourteenth century. The church is full of monuments, the finest being that of Edward, Lord Stourton, who died in 1535. Beside him lies his wife Agnes.

Stourhead

The Stourtons had connections with this place from Saxon times until the Hoares came in the late seventeenth century. In 1448 Sir John Stourton, a former High Sheriff of Wiltshire, was created the first Lord Stourton by Henry VI. In the seventeenth century the eighth baron was hanged in Salisbury market-place for the murder of two men both called Hartgill, which somewhat tainted the family name.

In 1720 the first Henry Hoare acquired the property and pulled down the old Stourton House in order to build his new Stourhead. It is a splendid building and its beauty is enhanced by the magnificent collection of Chippendale furniture, some of which was made by Chippendale on the premises. The house and gardens are now owned and cared for by the National Trust (see TIC and NT), and as the Trust has produced excellent guides to the property, there is no need to elaborate further. Instead, let us turn to the visionary and creator of the famous garden, Henry Hoare II.

Visionary he must have been, for only he could visualize the garden as it is today. Few trees that he planted had reached maturity by the time of his death. Although he maintained an interest in his business affairs, his family and his garden were his whole life. Ironically his most productive years were during times of tragedy and death within the family. So many of his hopes and dreams were for his family, and one by one they died, leaving only Richard Colt Hoare, a nephew, as his successor. How glad Henry must have been to know that Stourhead was to be left in the capable hands of that great antiquary and historian.

Henry Hoare came from a family of London bankers, the business having been established about 1672 by his grandfather Richard. In 1718, after the death of Richard, Henry's father bought the manor of Stourton and in this way turned his wealth into power by purchasing land which would raise him both socially and politically. The house Henry's father built and called Stourhead was in the Palladian style which was becoming fashionable at that time, and this no doubt brought further social acknowledgement. This was the time of the Grand Tours which the wealthy undertook, travelling the continent in order to become cultured and knowledgeable, particularly in the visual arts. The great Italian architect Palladio and his buildings with their classical lines were greatly admired and successfully emulated in this country.

Henry's father died in 1725, soon after Stourhead was completed, and in 1741 Henry came to live there. Known as Henry the Magnificent to his family, he was tall and elegant, an excellent horseman, a good shot and 'well-versed in polite literature'. He was wealthy and seemed at the 'height of fortune'. But in two years his second wife Susan died, leaving him with a son and two daughters. It was then that he began on his garden in earnest.

We know much of the doings of Henry Hoare through his prolific letter-writing. Many of his thoughts and hopes went down on paper, particularly to his daughter Susanna and his granddaughter Harriet. It seems that the family contributed to the layout of the garden, for in 1762 Henry wrote to Susanna telling her of the stone bridge:

You always wished I would build at the passage to the orchard & the scheme of carrying the water up and losing out of sight towards the parish. The Bridge is now about. It is simple & plain. I took it from Palladios Bridge at Vicenze, 5 arches, & when you stand at the Pantheon the water will be seen thro the Arches & it will look as if the River came thro the village & that this was the Village Bridge for publick use; The View of the

Bridge, Village & Church altogether will be a Charming Gaspard picture at that end of the water.

He took great delight in riding, walking and exploring on his estate with his grandchildren, often referring to them as 'the dear children'. He usually ended his letters with concern for the family's health.

His inclusion of the Bristol High Cross in his landscape afforded much discussion. The citizens of Bristol had regarded the cross as 'a ruinous and superstitious relick' and 'a public nuisance'. In 1764 Henry was present with the pieces, which had lain in the cathedral crypt for two years, and they were transported to Stourhead in six wagons. The following year Henry wrote to Lord Bruce, Susanna's husband: 'The Cross is now in hand & there are so many pieces that we must I believe employ Harriet to put it together as she is such an adept in joyning the map of the Countys of England'.

Henry remained interested in his project until his seventies. His health allowed him to take long rides particularly to Savernake, the home of Lord Bruce and Susanna. Here he gave advice on the improvement of Savernake Forest. But eventually in his old age Stourhead became 'more Pain than Pleasure', and having made over his property to his nephew Richard Colt Hoare, his son having died at the age of 21, he retired to his villa Flitcroft in Clapham, and there, outliving Susanna by a year, died in 1785 at the age of 80. His memorial in the church at Stourton has the following inscription:

> Ye who have viewed in Pleasure's choicest hour,
> The earth embellish'd on these banks of Stour,
> With grateful Reference to this Marble lean,
> Rais'd to the Friendly founder of the Scene,
> Here with pure love of smiling Nature warm'd,
> This far-fam'd Demy-Paradise be form'd:
> And, happier still, here learn'd from Heaven to find
> A sweeter Eden in a bounteous Mind.
> Thankful these fair and flowery paths be trod,
> And priz'd them only as they lead to GOD

From *The Stourhead Landscape* by Kenneth Woodbridge (National Trust, 1971).

THE WYLYE VALLEY

Between the towns of Warminster and Salisbury lies the once marsh-filled valley of the Wylye. It is sandwiched between two almost parallel roads. One is the fast and somewhat hazardous A36 on the north side of the river and the other to the south winds peacefully through the little villages on the banks of the river. The downs to the north are an archaeologist's paradise, having revealed some of the richest finds in the county, much of it from the Bronze Age. Knook Castle on Knook Down was a fort of three and a half acres, and probably belongs to the Iron Age. One mile west of Knook Castle is Knook Barrow, an unchambered long barrow. The Romans also left their mark in the area with roads and settlements. Knook itself was also once a Roman camp.

Tour 19: Villages north of the river

Heytesbury lies three miles to the east of Warminster. In the last months of 1986 the village was by-passed and the A36 now runs north of the village thrusting its way through the parkland of Heytesbury House. The village has undoubtedly benefited, so has the motorist, who not only can go faster but can also catch sight of the mansion with its long plain front of 1782 concealing an earlier building of the previous century, flanked by its magnificent parkland trees, a sight previously denied to the village traffic. However, I have sympathy for the occupants of the house who now look out on traffic and a park divided in two.

Heytesbury is an ancient borough with a wealth of history and it is worth taking the old road in order to see it. This was Hungerford territory – that famous family who sprang to prominence in the fourteenth century, increasing their wealth through the acquisition of land and the purchase of manors, one of which was Heytesbury,

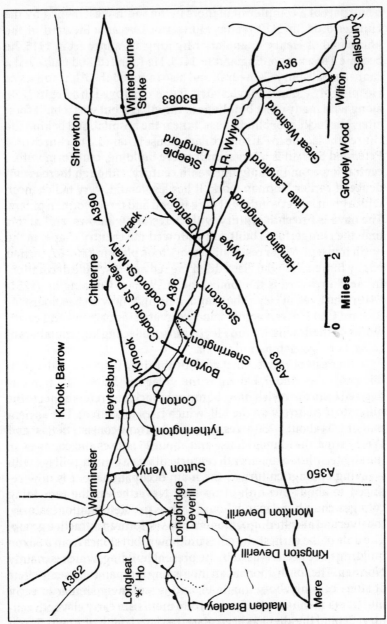

Tours 19, 20, and 21: The Wylye Valley

being part of a complex of manors in the south-west owned by the Hungerfords. In 1419 Walter Hungerford became Steward of the household of Henry V, and after fighting at Agincourt in 1415, he became Treasurer of England in 1428. He founded and endowed a chapel in Salisbury Cathedral, and also founded the Almshouses or Hospital of St John in Heytesbury. It was destroyed in a fire in 1770, along with many other buildings in the village, but was rebuilt soon after. The lockup, or blind house, is near the hospital, and behind the church the Jacobean Parsonage Farmhouse is found. The church of St Peter and St Paul is a large, impressive building, cruciform with a central tower and mainly thirteenth century, although there is evidence of earlier Norman work. It has a splendid, very tall chancel, with a great lancet window at the east end and three Norman pillars. The nave is fifteenth century with clerestory windows, and at this time the Hungerfords built and endowed the chantry chapel in the north transept. Major restoration work took place in 1864-67, carried out by Butterfield who also added the red and black tile decoration. In the churchyard is the tombstone of William Cunnington (1754-1810) who lived in Heytesbury and, with his fellow archaeologist Sir Richard Colt Hoare, explored and excavated the barrows and earthworks on the downs around Heytesbury, collecting huge numbers of coins, bones, skeletons and fossils.

A mile east of Heytesbury, close by the river at the foot of the great hill known as Knook Down, is the village of **Knook**. Its name is derived from the Welsh *cnwc*, bump or hillock, and refers either to the hill or to the barrow on the hill, which rises to 621 feet. The ancient manor was about 1,250 acres in extent, but now consists of East and West Farms, the Manor House and about 25 houses and cottages. In the eighteenth and nineteenth centuries it was a thriving village with weaving and agriculture as the main occupations, but is now reduced to about one-fifth of its size. Nevertheless the remaining cottages, church and manor house with its pre-Reformation features, the river and a scattering of modern houses, form an attractive group. The date of the earliest church is unknown, but stones from a Saxon building have been re-used in the present building, which is mainly Norman. The south door has an interesting tympanum, a semi-circle of stone carving about the lintel, and is strikingly similar to early illustrated manuscripts. The intricate motifs are early eleventh century. Behind the alter has been placed a short length of Anglo-Saxon interlace band. Note two beautifully carved Norman capitals on either side of the chancel arch. The church was restored in 1874-6 by Butterfield.

Walk down the lane past the church and over the little bridge. There is a tantalizing walk from here across the fields to Corton about a mile away. **Corton** itself is a pretty village of thatched garden walls, seventeenth century cottages and some larger houses. Take the lane which follows a circular route round the village and back across the meadows to Knook.

Further east along the A36 is **Codford St Peter**. This is a must for those interested in Saxon work, for in the church can be found one of the most fascinating pieces of Saxon sculpture in the country. The church, on the busy main road, contains one of Wiltshire's treasures - part of a ninth century carved stone cross, wonderfully preserved, showing a man with a mallet in his hand standing by a tree with his head thrown back and reaching for the fruit. It seems to depict midsummer festivities associated with the extensive

Saxon sculpture, Codford St Peter

marshes which used to fill the Wylye valley.

Further east again is **Codford St Mary** where an ancient bridge spans the river (now bypassed) and where it is possible to paddle and picnic. **Fisherton de la Mere** is a tiny hamlet with a lovely old mill house and thatched cottages near the church, which looks out over the meadows. At Deptford take the A303 north towards Winterbourne Stoke, and in a couple of miles turn left for Chitterne.

Chitterne

Chitterne is a small oasis in a valley in the midst of the chalkland plains. For some decades its remote position led to a reduction in its population, but with approximately 220 residents it has remained stable for some time. Past the Victorian church of flint and stone runs a winterbourne stream, so named as it flows only in winter. These streams are often found in chalk and limestone districts, the best known being the river Bourne in the south-east of the county and where we find a group of Winterbourne-named villages. In Chitterne a small bridge opposite the church gives access to a large open playing-field with good equipment for children. The village was once split into the two parishes of All Saints and St Mary's. The church of All Saints was rebuilt in 1863, and its solid tower dominates that part of the village. Built as a Perpendicular church, it is known more for its memorials than for its architecture. One memorial describes at length the life of Matthew Mitchell of Chitterne Manor, who went to sea at the age of eight in 1718 and retired as Commodore in 1747. The chancel of St Mary's with its lovely tracery is all that is left of the medieval Perpendicular church which stands near the Manor House. Chitterne House, north of the parish church, is a seventeenth century house of flint and stone, and stands behind a wide imposing gateway.

A sign forbidding tanks to enter the road to the church reminds the visitor of the nature of the business taking place on the nearby Plain. Due to a decision made at the beginning of 1987 Chitterne is to be the unfortunate neighbour of a 'German' village which is to be built on the downs nearby. This extremely controversial decision by the army and planning authorities for FIBUA (fighting in built up areas) training activities will, in the words of a local councillor, provide 'many hours of concentrated noise but these villages, being so close to the training area now, should be able to live with it.' Poor Chitterne.

Tour 20: *Villages south of the river*

At each end of the Wylye Valley is a great house. At the eastern end, where the river is reinforced by the Nadder before pouring into the Avon at Salisbury, is Wilton House (*see* TIC). At the western end, slightly north of the source of the Wylye, is Longleat House (*see* TIC). Both houses are of extreme interest and are open to the public.

Between these two great mansions are some of the most lovely of Wiltshire's villages close by a fisherman's paradise, the Wylye river.

Travelling north-west from Wilton on the A36, cross the Wylye at **Great Wishford**. An oak tree stands in the village near the flagpole, and under the tree meetings of the Wishford Oak Apple Club were held in the last century to ensure the immemorial rights of residents to cut and gather firewood in Grovely Wood above the village. The ancient custom stems from the festival of the green woods which became known as Oak Apple Day. Great Wishford still celebrates the festival. If you are in Salisbury Cathedral on Oak Apple Day, you may hear the shout of 'Grovely! Grovely! and all Grovely' raised by the villagers as they lay their offerings of great oak boughs before the altar.

The thirteenth century church of St Michael has many interesting memorials, one of which is to Sir Richard Grobham, lord of the manor at Wishford in the sixteenth century, and the builder of the group of almshouses near the church. Sir Thomas Bonham also has a memorial in the church. Although married he was not much of a family man, and when his wife gave birth to a set of twins he thought it preferable to go off to the Holy Land on a Crusade. Time passed and he returned. Within a year his wife produced more children – this time septuplets! They were all carried to the church in a sieve to be christened. The brass figures of the nine children are set in the memorial, although some have since disappeared; so has the sieve, which hung there for centuries.

Hanging Langford enjoys the peace of the south side of the river, while its neighbour, **Steeple Langford**, with its interesting church, lies across the stream-strewn meadows near the A36, and now by-passed. Another village that has been successfully by-passed is **Wylye**, which until 1977 also used to bear the brunt of constant traffic; and travellers to and from the West Country became acquainted with its narrow lanes with such names as Teapot Street and Sheepwash Lane. It is an attractive village with the Wylye river running quietly under the old bridge and the mill house nearby. On the banks of the river is a children's playground and a pleasant place for a picnic; from here it is a short walk to the church. St Mary's was mainly rebuilt in 1844-6, but retains its Early English chancel window of three-stepped lancet and dogtooth decoration. The pub next to the church has a good atmosphere and an attractive small courtyard garden.

Stockton has a great variety of buildings including thatched estate cottages of half-timber and stone, and some laced with chequered flint. Along a gravel drive to the south is Long Hall, with its mixture of timber framing and an elegant Georgian front. Nearby is a Victorian school and flower-bedecked cottages. Parallel to this lane is the way to the church. In the cottage with the handsome porch near the church lived Anne Raxworthy, a retired lady's maid who always dressed in a black silk gown to go to church. Humbled by her imminent death, she asked to be buried where people would tread on her. As you enter the church look down, for there is her gravestone, worn by countless feet.

The church of St John Baptist has Norman arcades and the nave is separated from the Early English chancel by a thick wall pierced by two side openings and a little arch. There is a fine memorial to John Topp (*see* below), his wife and children. There is an effigy of an unknown lady of the fourteenth century lying on her side, and another monument (1704) to a son of Stockton, Henry Greenhill, who became a Governor of the Gold Coast and finished his days founding and building the Royal Dockyard at Plymouth. The roof of the church is made from the cargo of a ship that was wrecked off the Isle of White. Bishop Wilberforce, who was then the local curate, helped in the rescue, and the grateful crew gave him the cedarwood from the ship's hold.

The Topp Almshouses, which were founded in 1641, are reached up another side turning near the church. A charming group of stone buildings, they are set on three sides of a forecourt, and were built by the rich cloth merchant, John Topp, who also built the fine Elizabethan Stockton House which is found amid parkland at the west end of the village. Close to its gates is Manor Farmhouse, built in 1596, the home of Jerome Poticary, an ancestor of Henry Greenhill and himself a clothier. His monument is also found in the church.

Sherrington is a village on a loop below the road through the valley. It has made use of the streams which descend to its meadows by creating a large pond for growing watercress, although this is now no longer in production. The best way to see the village is to leave the car and walk around the loop, past the fields with Jacob sheep and down to the lane with the thatched wall which leads to the river. For a longer walk, the bridge and the path on the other side leads to **Codford**. The church and its adjacent thatched rectory stand near the arm of a moat, and the manor farm opposite was once the site of a castle owned by the Giffards in early medieval times. The church has an unusual dedication to S.S.Cosmos and Damian. A picture in the chancel tells the story of the two saints:

> These saints are said to have been twin Arabian physicians martyred for their Christian Faith on 17th September, 301 A.D. They became the Patron Saints of the Medici, of Medicine and of Travellers; and a 13th Century Crusader built this our own Church as a thank offering for his home-coming. Only four English Churches have this dedication. The Church of S.S.Cosmos and Damian in Rome is built over a Temple of the Heavenly Twins. Legend says that the Saints substituted the diseased leg of a man who prayed in their Church of San Pietro in Vincoli in Rome. The black leg can be seen in this picture.

Boyton has greater connections with the Giffard family, especially the church. Two of them, Walter Archbishop of York and Godfrey Bishop of Worcester, both of whom became Lord Chancellors of England, built a unique chapel in memory of their parents. The church is approached along an elegant driveway lined with a sea of daffodils in spring. The tower entrance is through a massive Early English arch with fine mouldings. The chancel and south chapel are

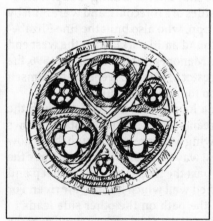

Giffard Chapel, Boyton church

also Early English, and the north chapel is Decorated with a good example of reticulated tracery of that period. But the west window of the Giffard chapel is of especial interest. Nicklaus Pevsner describes it thus: 'The w. window is a tour-de-force...a large circular window with three quatrefoil spherical triangles and between them three circles each filled by three small circles. Bar tracery appears at Salisbury Cathedral only about

Sherrington, Wylye Valley

1270 and the tracery here is a little in advance of Salisbury. One might date the chapel *c.*1280...' As he says, no architectural traveller will forget Boyton.

Tytherington is a farming community which has become reduced in size in recent times but retains a very special feature – its church. This single-cell chapel has sat on its grassy knoll by the bend in the road since 1083. The board outside states it was endowed by the Empress Mathilda, mother of Henry II, in 1140. The bell hanging in the little turret is also of great antiquity.

Tour 21: *The Deverills*

These villages can be visited while enjoying the places already mentioned along the Wylye valley. However, to appreciate them more fully, and perhaps explore the superb downland which rises above them, more time should be allowed.

Drive south from Warminster on the A350 and watch for the sign to Shear Water. Situated on the southern edge of the Longleat Estate in dense woodland this attractive lake was made in 1791 and is used for sailing and other water activities. Woodland paths run close by the lake and criss-cross the forest where a longer hike to the northwest will bring the walker to Park Hill to gaze down on the magnificence of Longleat House and its Safari Park (*see* TIC).

Continue on the road south from **Shear Water** to join the road signposted to Maiden Bradley. Within half a mile the road crosses a track (marked on map). The track to the left is one of the approaches to the splendid ridges of downland where the ancient Britons spent so much of their time. On Cold Kitchen Hill enormous quantities of objects have been found from early Iron Age to Roman times. High on the ridge there is evidence of a Roman temple or shrine although all that remains is a circular heap of unploughed land. On Cow Hill the discovery of the post holes of three large circular houses has provided evidence of occupation from the seventh to the second centuries BC. Smaller earthworks still survive as do long barrows and burial mounds. From these chalk ridges, one of the highest points in the county, where larks soar and sing and harebells grow, there are panoramic views of all that is best of the English countryside.

Nearby **Horningsham** is a straggling village with its houses dotting the hillside and valley. It is strangely un-unified and a mile separates the little chapel one end and the entrance to the great house the other. Near the inn between the two are the Twelve Apostles and the Four Disciples. These are the names given to two remarkable groups of lime trees, their branches dividing and spreading like the vaulting in a cathedral. The little Meeting House in Chapel Street is said to have been built by Sir John Thynne in 1566-7 for the Scottish Presbyterian workmen who were brought from Scotland to build Longleat House. These artisans lived nearby in a place still called Little Scotland. However recent research does not confirm the date of the chapel and it is now thought to have been built around 1700.

Turn left at the Thynne Arms taking the road to **Maiden Bradley**. Here in the twelfth century a hospital was founded by Margaret Bissett for leper maidens and two of the buildings, at Priory Farm, still survive. Bradley House with its imposing gateway was the home of the Seymours and was built about 1700. In the nineteenth century it was largely demolished leaving one wing which is still occupied. An elaborate memorial to Sir Edward Seymour is found in the church, a building noted also for its windows. In the south-east of the south aisle are fragments from the fourteenth and sixteenth centuries and there is part of a picture of fourteenth century harvesters. In the east window is the conversion of St Paul and in the north aisle a window full of colour from this century by Christopher Whall. In the village the Post Office Stores is from the seventeenth century with a late Elizabethan fireplace, being first a private house and then an inn. The fountain in the village street was provided by the Duke of Somerset in 1891 and is a reminder of life before the motor-car:

> *Drink, travellers, drink of Bradley's purest rill*
> *Which, strange to say, runs quite a mile up hill;*
> *Then to your panting steeds let all attend*
> *An honest horse is surely man's best friend.*

Find the road east to **Kingston Deverill**. Here a large house has been turned into luxury holiday apartments and in the attractive grounds amongst the campers are a heap of sarsen stones brought down from the hills to commemorate, it is believed, a stop made by Alfred the Great before his great battle against the Danes. The River Wylye (or is this the River Deverill?) is little more than a stream as it gurgles under a tiny stone bridge by a village garden. The church has a fifteenth century tower and two arches of the previous century in the nave. The rest was rebuilt in 1846.

Follow the stream north on the Warminster Road (B3095) to **Monkton Deverill**. The tiny hamlet is on a loop with the church, with its ancient tower in the middle. It was rebuilt in 1845, rededicated to Alfred the Great in 1850 and declared redundant in 1970.

Sarsen stones, Kingston Deverill

A couple of miles north, **Brixton Deverill** hides up a small road opposite the river. The thirteenth century church stands by a group of thatched cottages and Manor Farmhouse with its old mullioned windows. At the end of the road past the farm buildings, a track will take the walker up the hill to a tumulus at Beech Clump and down again to the church.

The five Deverills were named after the compound Welsh-English word *Dobroial* meaning cultivated water field and the application of the word is obvious on the stretch of river between Hill

Deverill and Longbridge Deverill. The river has been channelled into a series of wide ponds for the local industry of watercress cultivation. At **Hill Deverill**, as the road widens, a track to the left leads to Manor Farm, a seventeenth century building with an extremely long barn attached to the east side. In the farmyard is a T-shaped building with a surviving window with four arched lights. The church has a bellcote and was rebuilt in 1843.

Finally to **Longbridge Deverill** which sits astride the A350. Its most attractive feature is the group of Thynne Almshouses which was founded in 1655 by Sir James Thynne of Longleat. They stand above the Wylye and close by the early Norman church with its many later additions. Here lies Sir John Thynne, builder of Longleat House, who died in 1580.

THE VALE OF PEWSEY

The Vale of Pewsey is roughly 12 miles long by no more than five miles across north to south. It is bordered by hills on three sides, the most impressive being to the north, where the great Wansdyke, or Woden's Ditch, was built sometime after the Roman occupation, to repel early Saxon invaders. Here too are found the rounded hills of Martinsell, Huish, Knap Hill, Milk Hill and Tan Hill. The last rises 962 feet above sea level, and from it can be seen Salisbury's cathedral spire 25 miles away to the south. Here runs Tan Hill Way affording glorious views and peace, although for many hundreds of years it was the noisy scene of an annual sheep and cattle fair.

This unspoilt downland has exceptionally rich farm land. William Cobbett, who visited it in the 1820s, spent some time calculating the vast wool, wheat and animal productions, declaring that it would be enough to provide 'bread for 800 families, mutton for 500 and bacon and beer for 207.' He also said it would 'be impossible to find a more beautiful and pleasant country than this.'

The villages of the Vale have found fame in the well known Moonrakers' tale. Two local men were found by Excise men one night raking the surface of a pond. When asked their business they replied, pointing to the reflection of the moon, that they were trying to retrieve 'thik gurt yaller cheese'. The Excise men rode away laughing at such fools, while the two men raked deeper and pulled out their hidden kegs of brandy!

Tour 22: North of the Kennet and Avon Canal

At the west end of the Vale, **Bishops Cannings** lies just north of an attractive and navigable section of the Kennet and Avon Canal. The tall church spire draws you to this village of thatched cottages

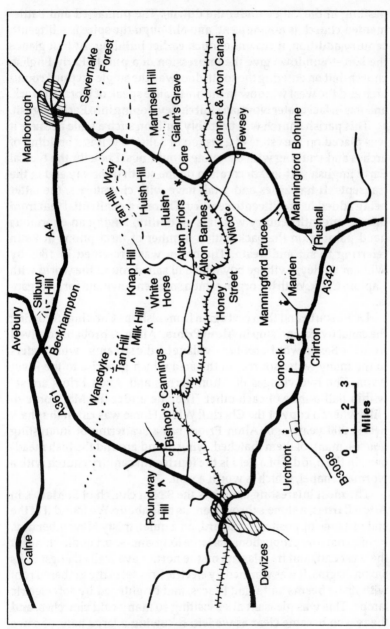

Tours 22 and 23: The Vale of Pewsey

nestling in the valley under the downs. The pinnacled and battle-mented church is magnificent, and although the spire is a fifteenth century addition, it crowns a much earlier building. At first glance the lancet windows give the impression of a purely Early English church, but on entering the south doorway the single-stepped round arch and the west window in the north aisle speak of Norman work, and it is in fact a later Norman church developing into Early English.

This parish church was probably built on such a scale because it was placed on the estate of a bishop of Salisbury. It is a building of arches and vaulting with elaborate mouldings. Look for the typical Early English stiff-leaf decoration on the south doorway and in the transepts. It has aisles and a tall nave with clerestories, the latter being added in the fifteenth century. There is a penitential seat from the seventeenth century which is an oddity, having an enormous hand painted on the back with a number of inscriptions in Latin referring to sin and death. The organ was presented in 1809 by William Bayley, a village boy who had sailed round the world with Captain Cook. With the organ came a small endowment for an organist.

Drive south and then east again from Bishops Cannings, crossing the canal twice, and stop in **Alton Priors**. 'Alton' is probably derived from the Saxon word *awel-tun* – village by the streams – which refers to the many water sources in the area which give rise to the River Avon. The two villages of Alton Barnes and Alton Priors are set within half-a-mile of each other. They lie under the Marlborough Hills where a copy of the Cherhill White Horse was cut in the chalk nearly 200 years ago. Alton Priors has a scattering of interesting houses, many of them thatched, lying in and around the lush meadows. In the middle of a field is the fourteenth century church with a Norman chapel, which is worth a visit.

The most interesting church is the Saxon church of St Mary's in **Alton Barnes**, a stone's throw from its neighbour. We found it at the end of a lane opposite a farmyard, on a quiet, misty November day. Its high narrow proportions, its large long-and-short quoin stones at the west end, and its pilasters on the north nave wall all attest to its Saxon origins. It was warmed by electric fires set in the timbered roof with its tie beams and wind braces, and brightened by soft electric lamps. This was pleasant after visiting so many cold churches, and the reason became clear as we left: following a large herd of cows heading for the farm across the way came a straggling party of

Alton Barnes

churchgoers. The central figure was a wide-eyed baby in long white robes carried by a proud father. What a delightful place in which to be christened!

Come back out of the lane and turn left; drive a few hundred yards to **Honey Street**. This is the name given to the wharf on the Kennet and Avon Canal. It is still an interesting place, although some of the older weatherboarded buildings have gone. On the other side of the canal, follow the lane to The Barge – a pub with accommodation and food for weary towpath walkers or canoeists, and a pleasant place to sit for a drink.

Return to the crossroads at Alton Barnes and take the Wilcot road and then the turning to Stowell for the A345 Pewsey to Marlborough road. Turn left towards Marlborough and here the village of **Oare** sits astride the main road. It is associated with the name of Clough Williams Ellis, the architect and creator of the famous Italian village of Portmeirion in North Wales. He it was who added the symmetrical wings to **Oare House** (open for NGS; *see* Gardens Open), a small mansion built in 1740 by a rich London wine merchant. Another house in the village known as Cold Blow, and a row of thatched cottages, were also designed by Clough Williams Ellis.

North of the village is Rainscombe House, magnificently situated below Oare Hill. A quarter of a mile east of Oare, on top of **Martinsell**

Hill, is Giant's Grave, an Iron Age promontory of two-and-a-half acres. At the top of the long hill out of Oare there is a parking area and footpath which will take you around the ridge of Martinsell Hill and up to the fort, a particularly worthwhile walk of just over a mile. Martinsell Hill can also be approached on foot from the centre of the village. Just south of the Post Office is a small road, at the end of which a sign will direct the walker to the foot of the hill.

From Oare drive direct to Marlborough for a cream tea in a cafe in the High street, or branch off to the left a few miles north of Oare, signposted to Manton or Clatford, to join the A4 west of Marlborough. After passing Silbury Hill on your right, join the A361 for Devizes, where the Wiltshire Downs stretch away into the distance.

Tour 23: South of the Kennet and Avon Canal

Wilcot, a mile or two north-west of Pewsey, straddles the canal with thatched cottages either side of the bridge. South of the green and the canal is the original village. Turn right at the Inn and at the end of the road, past more thickly thatched cottages with names such as Bread Oven Cottage, you will find the church, manor house and farm buildings. Wilcot Manor and its long-gone vineyards are mentioned in Domesday. In 1737 a circular dovecot, similar to the one at Avebury, was built in the grounds, and can be seen over the churchyard wall. There was a church here in Norman times, and the chancel arch is late Norman. Unfortunately the building was partly destroyed by fire and rebuilt after 1876. In the chancel is a plaque in memory of the son of Admiral Sir John Gore who lost his life at sea in 1835 trying to rescue a sailor during a storm.

The canal towpath is particularly attractive on this stretch near Wilcot, and a short walk south-west of Wilcot will bring you to **Ladies Bridge**, an unusually ornate bridge designed by Rennie in 1808. Walking north-east and near Stowell Park, a mansion completed in 1813, you will pass some attractive cottages in brick and thatch. Starting at Honey Street, and walking the towpath to Pewsey Wharf, located north of Pewsey on the A345 – a distance of about four miles – is one of the most delightful and interesting sections of the entire canal.

Return from the church to the crossroads at the inn and take the Manningford road south. There is Manningford Bruce, Manningford

Ladies Bridge, Kennet and Avon Canal, near Wilcot

Abbots and Manningford Bohune, and it is difficult to relate the right
church to the right village. Try and find the church at **Manningford
Bruce**, as it is a perfectly preserved Norman building and worth a
visit. From the centre of the village, drive half-a-mile south to the
A345 and turn right. Almost immediately turn right again up a small
lane. The church is at the end. It is of flint, laid consistently in
herringbone pattern. Its form is typically Norman and consists of
nave, chancel and apse. There are two original rounded windows
with deep splay in the apse and one in the nave. The two doors are
rounded and plain, but the Norman chancel arch has much ornamentation. In 1882 a wagon roof was built over the nave, and an attractive
herringbone pattern in parquet boards the ceiling and apse, perhaps
echoing the external herringbone pattern.

The plaque on the chancel wall has an attractive coat of arms and

Manningford Bruce

is in memory of Mary Nicholas who, with her sister, helped King Charles II to escape after the Battle of Worcester. Jane Lane, Mary's sister, rode on the back of the King's horse dressed as a groom, and led him to safety through the unwary Parliamentary troops who were hunting him. The family's arms now include the three lions of England, a rare privilege granted by the King in gratitude for his deliverance. The fields around Manningford are given to the cultivation of daffodils and tulips; spring is an obvious time to visit the area.

Return to the A345 and turning right, drive to **Rushall**. Take the pleasant A345 road west through the vale to **Chirton**. This is a village of thatched houses and thatched walls, well-cut grass edges and lovely Georgian buildings. In the vicinity is **Conock**, which has two manor houses. Conock Old Manor is of brick, and was built about 1710; **Conock Manor** (garden open for NGS and GS; *see* Gardens Open) was built of brick and stone in the mid-eighteenth century, and has a golden cupola on the stables which can be seen shining across the fields. The church of St John Baptist at Chirton is at the end of the long village street and sits on a mound amid a beautifully tended churchyard, from where there is a splendid view looking north.

The stone church is extremely pleasing inside and out, and the rounded arches of the Normans are much in evidence. The doorway on the south side has lavish carving on continuous zigzags, and the Norman ornamental motif of beakheads is interspersed with odd hands, heads and beasts. The immediate door surround is of the fourteenth century; note that this section has a pointed apex to the arch. Although rather over-restored in 1850, the interior has fine, late Norman arcades and a Norman chancel arch. The font is also Norman, with statuettes of the 12 apostles under arches. One of the finest features of the church is its magnificent single framed timber roof, which is believed to be the original one erected by the Normans. The information leaflet with coloured illustrations giving the history of the church and its parish is well worth buying.

Return down the village street and take the left turn through the lanes to **Marden**, another village of thatched cottages and barns, and Marden Manor House, built in the early nineteenth century. To the north-east of the village is a late neolithic earthwork with a surrounding bank and inner ditch known as a henge, covering 35 acres, bordered on the other side by the River Avon. When excavated in 1969, it produced many interesting artefacts including flints and antler picks.

All Saints is a Norman church. It has a lavish doorway and an exquisite Norman chancel arch with scalloped capitals and zigzags in the arch. The pinnacled tower with a stair turret is 500 years old. The buttresses have attractive rare pinnacles ornamented with small projections called crockets. Imagine this rather dark church lit by candles, and it would warm the hardest heart!

VILLAGES OF THE PLAIN

The great central plateau of Salisbury Plain is a vast undulating stretch of chalk downland which runs from Urchfont and the Lavingtons to Salisbury in a north/south direction, and from Westbury to Ludgershall west/east. The turf of the chalk down is ideal for the grazing of sheep and in times past gave sustenance to huge flocks.

Large tracts of the Plain are now given over to military use and in some places the character of the Plain has been changed by this intrusion. However, it has been as much changed by agriculture as by the appurtenances of war and much of it has come under the plough never to revert to its verdant pasture. But the Plain still dominates the county with its glorious scenery where the skylarks sing above abundant downland flowers; an ancient land full of mystery and sense of space where our prehistoric past is everywhere visible with barrows, camps, dykes, lynchets or 'shepherd steps' all showing intense activity and occupation from a remote period. Finally, the chalk downs provide an ideal landscape for Wiltshire's seven white horses carved on the side of the steep ridges.

Tour 24: Imber and Villages of the River Till

The road from Devizes to Salisbury enters the Plain near West Lavington before crossing the Ridgeway at St Joan a Gore's Cross. Opposite a huge barn with a thatch like hair that has grown too long, a track leads over the desolate down to **Imber**. 'Seven miles from any town, Imber, Imber on the down' is a local couplet. The village is now derelict, its inhabitants having been required to leave by the army during the 1939-45 war in order to have a battle- practice ground. At that time all access by the public was forbidden. Things are a little more relaxed now and on highdays and holidays public access is allowed.

Imber

In a hollow in the Plain the visitor will find a scene of desolation that was once Imber. The church on the hill, more or less intact but boarded up, sits amid its churchyard of broken tombs, brightened only by a couple of bunches of fresh flowers left by an anonymous relative. Below the church the 'village' is one of concrete block buildings depicting the Post Office, butcher, baker, haberdashers, etc., some with phoney Irish names for their proprietors. One, with a touch of irony, has Job Centre in bold lettering. All have been erected for urban warfare purposes. Towards the end of the village a large old building, now completely fenced off with boards and barbed wire, stands below empty farm buildings and is a reminder of more prosperous times. Mud, puddles and a stream which floods the concrete road completes the picture of desolation. It is hard to believe that parts of the church date back to the thirteenth century. Imber was home for generations of people now long gone but some of whom live elsewhere and visit their former village when they can. Imber can also be approached from Heytesbury to the south.

Continue across the plain from St Joan a Gore Cross to the village of **Tilshead**. In wet winters water from the springs on the Plain nearby descends to increase the volume of the little River Till to the south. Tilshead is so called, not because it is the head of the Till, but

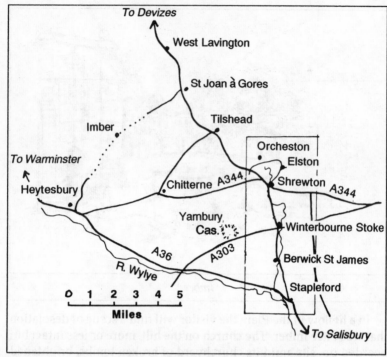

Tour 24: Imber and the villages of the River Till

because it derives from 'Tidwulf's hide', Tidwulf being a Saxon farmer. How confusing! It is a small place now but at the time of the Domesday survey it was active and prosperous and was one of the largest boroughs in Wiltshire, no doubt due mainly to large-scale sheep-farming in the area.

The Normans built a church here with arcades of three bays and arches that had no moulding or decoration at all. Pevsner wonders if the arcades are 'especially early or especially far from civilisation?' The Early English chancel is particularly fine with stepped lancets in the east window. The main street is attractive with thatched houses and much flint and chequerwork in the buildings. The surrounding neighbourhood abounds with tumuli and other earthworks. A long barrow called White Barrow, belonging to the National Trust, lies one mile to the south; it is 255 feet long and 156 feet wide. Another long barrow to the west known as The Old Ditch is 400 feet long, the largest in England.

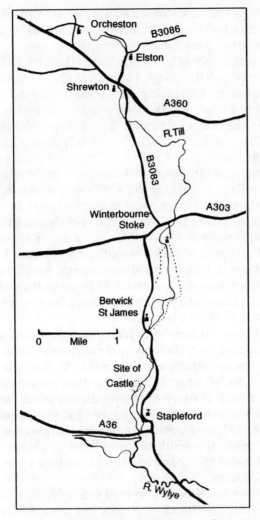

Tour 24: Detail of map opposite

The road passes over Orcheston Down. To the left of the road and below the down is the village of **Orcheston**. A double village with two churches it suffered greatly in 1841 during the 'Awful Visitation'. Normally rain is easily absorbed by the porous chalk but in this particular winter the villages of Tilshead, Orcheston, Shrewton and Winterbourne Stoke sustained terrible damage after heavy snow

123

thawed rapidly and little streams became torrents. In all, 47 houses as well as farm buildings were destroyed. Plaques on the houses commemorate the great flood.

Shrewton is a place of little bridges over the Till which normally runs quietly through the village. The round lock-up was moved back somewhat from its vulnerable position nearer the road after a tank had demolished it on more than one occasion. Shrewton consists of five parishes, the village being the hub with the parish fields extending from it like a wheel. The Catherine Wheel pub opposite the lock-up is aptly named.

At the south end of the village take the right turn to **Winterbourne Stoke**. The village sits astride the A303 and the church, the river, thatched cottages and some newer housing are found down the little road on the other side slightly to the east. The church has one of the most beautiful settings in Wiltshire. In spring, daffodils fill the extensive churchyard which looks south across the meadows with a thatched cottage and the River Till for company. A walk by the river, through the beechwoods to Berwick St James to the south is very worthwhile. A signpost by the church shows the way which can be a circular walk of about two miles.

In order to drive to **Berwick St James** leave the church and return to the A303 and turn left. Half way up the hill turn left onto the B3083. The village has an attractive main street with thatched roofs and gables and on the left, after the Boot Inn with its prominent boot pub sign, is the church. Through the Perpendicular porch the church is entered by a Norman doorway with green and white stone patterning. The interior is dominated by a fine thirteenth century chancel arch which spans the width of the chancel. A chalice of similar vintage which was in constant use here for centuries now resides in the British Museum.

The Till flows south beside the road to **Stapleford** where it joins the Wylye River. The church with some fine Norman work forms a delightful picture with a long row of newly thatched cottages and a white fence bordering the meadows. Stapleford Castle, now only a moated tree-covered mound, is found on the other side of the river at **Over Street**.

VILLAGES
IN THE SHADOW
OF THE PLAIN

Edington and Steeple Ashton lie within two miles of each other, and each has a great and beautiful church. It is interesting first to visit Edington Priory and then Steeple Ashton, as they are prime examples of how one architectural period develops and gives rise to the next. Edington, the earlier of the two, was built between 1352 and 1361, and shows perfectly the transition from the Decorated to the Perpendicular style of architecture in one glorious building. Steeple Ashton is 50 years later, and is pure Perpendicular.

Tour 25: Edington (and Westbury White Horse)

Edington lies east of Westbury in the shadow of a downland escarpment, a great hill which holds the secrets of the past. To the west is the village of Bratton, and on the hill above are the earthworks of Iron Age Bratton Castle. Close by is the oldest White Horse in the county, **Westbury White Horse**, which was cut in its present form in 1774, incorporated into the body of an earlier horse of uncertain age and origin. It is said that the earlier horse was cut to commemorate Alfred's victory over the Danes, but others will deny it. It is a romantic theory, and you are free to choose until new and undisputed evidence turns up. Hang gliders are now the horse's companions, but whether or not you are floating in the sky, the views stretching far to the Somerset hills are breathtaking.

Nestling in the hillside above the village of **Bratton** is one of the most charming churches in the county. The thirteenth century church with its fifteenth century tower is reached by a series of steps first plunging down one hill before ascending the next. There are traces of Norman architecture in the porch and transepts and the ceiling of the tower is vaulted in true fifteenth century style with carved floral bosses. This church should not be missed, and the climb may be

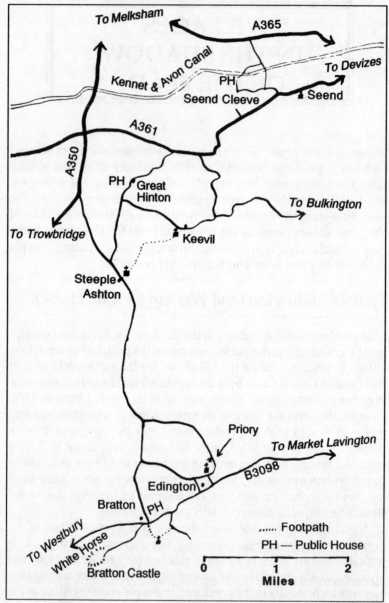

*Tours 25 & 26: Villages in the shadow of the Plain:
Edington and Steeple Ashton*

rewarded by a visit to The Duke, found in the centre of the village.

Half-a-mile to the east of Bratton is the village of **Edington**. One of Edington's sons, William of Edington, became Lord Chancellor and Bishop of Winchester, and his great interest in architecture included the rebuilding of Winchester Cathedral in the Gothic style and the founding of a Priory in his native village. Previously there had been a Norman church at Edington under the spiritual guidance of Romsey Abbey. Edward III was on the throne and his son the Black Prince had taken a particular interest in some French monks of an obscure Augustinian order called Bonshommes. William suggested that the monks be installed in his native village, where he personally supervised the pulling down of the old church and the building of the new priory. As was customary in such circumstances, the parishioners were given the use of the nave, and this was divided from the monastic chancel by a great screen. This rare wooden screen or pulpitum of 1500 still survives. The Priory is now the parish church with a multiple dedication to St Mary, St Katherine and All Saints.

The Priory was begun in 1352 just after the Black Death. This had so ravaged the population of England that it affected all walks of life, and in many places church building had been halted. When activity started again, plans were changed and new architectural styles evolved. All over the country the Decorated style of architecture with its elaborate tracery and flowing lines had reached the height of its success, and it was at this time that the Priory was begun. We still see the elaborate tracery in the windows but the more rectilinear appearance of the new Perpendicular style was being introduced. This is more apparent in the east chancel window, where the mullions reach in straight lines from the bottom of the window to the top.

The development of vaulting in our churches and cathedrals provides an indication of the date of particular architectural styles, and here at Edington the vaults and ceilings are of great interest. Excellent literature on this subject can be found in the church.

The church stands close to the monastic gardens, little of which remain except the walls and two huge yew trees which may have been there since the original Norman building. The cloisters and conventual buildings have gone, but the magnificent church that remains is almost unaltered except for careful restoration carried out between 1887 and 1891.

The nave is entered by the lofty vaulted south porch of three storeys. The beauty of the interior is stunning, the exquisite arches being topped by a pink and white plastered ceiling of the seventeenth century. The patterned floors are of dark and light marbles. Most of the window glass is clear, so the church is light and airy. The chancel, with its eighteenth century white plaster ceiling, is alive with sculpture in the Decorated style – mitred bishops, figures standing in elaborate fan-vaulted canopies and much small sculpture. Also in the chancel is a great seventeenth century monument to Lady Anne Beauchamp and her husband Sir Edward Lewis, who lived in the Priory House north of the church. She died in 1664. They lie in splendid clothes on beds of plaited straw, Lady Anne a little above her husband as befitted her rank. Kneeling below their parents are five children attended by angels.

The Chancel, Edington Church

The east window has already been mentioned, and the chancel side windows and transept windows are also a transition from one style to the other. The arches in the tracery are Decorated but the verticals in the upper arches are stressed and the top unit is completely Perpendicular. The west windows of the aisles and the clerestory are purely Decorated, but the west front with its double portal and eight light windows above show much that is Perpendicular.

In 1970 the York Glaziers Trust undertook the restoration of the East window of the north transept. Cleaning the medieval glass from this fourteenth century window involved the newest technology in glass restoration, including the use of ultra-sound vibrations. The glass was placed in a wire container and immersed in an ammonia-based solvent. The currents were transmitted through the liquid, resulting in a transformation of the glass with no harmful effects. The iron stanchions holding the glass had greatly added to its discoloration, and these have been replaced by manganese bronze, cut and shaped to the old design, thereby retaining the character of the window.

Edington has been fortunate in its Friends of the Priory who have worked tirelessly to raise money for continued restoration of this marvellous building. There is a fine carving by David Kindersley on the floor of the Lady Chapel to commemorate some recent restoration. Edington has become the setting for a celebrated annual music festival, with singers from cathedral and collegiate choirs from all over the country taking part. This no doubt would have delighted George Herbert, poet and music lover, whose monument can be seen in the reredos behind the chancel altar.

Tour 26: *Steeple Ashton and nearby villages*

The dominant feature of **Steeple Ashton** is its church, which rises up from the fields like an extravagantly decorated wedding cake. The High Street winds through a variety of delightful buildings, many of them timber-framed with brick infilling, some with symmetrical brick or stone fronts and dating from the seventeenth and eighteenth centuries. On the Green is an ancient octagonal lock-up with a domed roof, and the Village Cross, which dates back to 1679.

Nearby is Ashton House, which is older inside than its 1714 facade, and has an original fifteenth century hall with an open timber roof. In Vicarage Lane is the Old Parsonage, built of Bath stone in 1829, although parts of this building date back to the seventeenth century and even the fourteenth century. Here again the trusses and arch-braces in the timber roof of the hall survive. Back in the High Street we see more timber-framed houses, including the much-restored Market House.

Time and again visitors return to the splendid Perpendicular church of St Mary's. If you have visited Edington Priory, described in the previous section, you will be aware of the architectural features that were being introduced, to culminate in the last of the great medieval architectural styles between 1370 and 1550, and here at Steeple Ashton there is a superb example of the flowering of that style known as Perpendicular. The date of the original church is unknown, although the list of vicars goes back to 1252, and about that time a church was built. Around 1420 the tower was added, and 60 years later the old church, with the exception of the chancel and tower, was demolished to make way for the beautiful church seen today. In 1853 the Early English chancel was lengthened and the roof raised at the expense of the Master and Fellows of Magdalene College, Oxford.

As in so many other villages, the cloth-making industry brought much prosperity, and the clothiers set about the building of a new

Detail of lierne vaulting in the south porch – Steeple Ashton church

church, employing craftsmen of great ability. It is known that the north and south aisles were paid for by two clothiers, Robert Long and Walter Leucas, and the rest of the building by the parishioners. Wealthy they must have been, as the church was to have been stone-vaulted throughout – very ambitious for a village church. Unfortunately a fire destroyed part of the town, impoverishing the clothiers, and it was thought that at this time part of the nave vaulting collapsed. In 1670 the roof of the nave was again severely damaged in a storm by the falling spire which had topped the magnificent tower. While the spire was being rebuilt, another storm 'threw down the steeple and killed two men Labouring thereon...' Despite these disasters, the finished building with its pinnacles, flying buttresses, gargoyles, complicated vaulting patterns and splendid lofty interior is a sight not to be missed. Details of the architecture and the story of the church are explained in the booklet found within.

Steeple Ashton's proximity to Trowbridge, an important 'staple' market for wool and cloth, provided the villagers with a ready market for their products, but with the coming dependence on water power for the woollen mills, its demise was rapid. By the 1840s, mechanisation meant fewer jobs, especially for the unskilled labourer. Poverty, distress and despair were widespread throughout the country. As one Wiltshire woman put it, 'We don't live, we bides'. 'Poor relief' disappeared with the Poor Law Amendment Act, and instead of the needy receiving a weekly supplement and being housed in 'poor houses' in the village where they were born, they were sent to the newly opened workhouses in strange towns. Here men and women were separated and lost their dear-

Steeple Ashton

est possession – freedom. People went to great lengths to stay out of the workhouse.

Many young people decided to try for a better life abroad, and voyages to Australia and America became commonplace. America became a particularly attractive proposition after the first Mormons arrived in Trowbridge in 1844. The Church of England had provided little comfort or help for destitute families, supported as it was by landowners and employers who seemed short on compassion. The missionaries from the American Church of Latter-Day Saints came preaching that everyone had talents which should be used. Hope was given to those who joined them, and a new way of life in America was promised, and backed up by subsidised passages to the new land.

Between the 1840s and 1860s at least 60 out of 160 households in Steeple Ashton had a Mormon convert, and large parties of emigrants from the village and the surrounding area left for America. Perhaps they exchanged their native village for untold dangers and hardships – not least the voyage, during which so many died on board ship; at least they were free of the stifling English social structure. Many stayed with the church, others quarrelled with it, particularly on the issue of polygamy, and became farmers in the American mid-west.

Today, Steeple Ashton is a thriving village with much new housing – a pleasant place in which to live. Its long history is apparent in the many architectural styles of building. Time should be taken to explore the small side streets, discover buildings such as Old Chesils in Dark Lane, where the Mormons held meetings and which is still known as God's Corner, or the old granary which stands on its stone columns in the grounds of the Manor House past the church.

A mile-and-a-half as the crow flies, north-east of Steeple Ashton, lies **Keevil**. This village of thatched cottages and great houses can be reached on foot over the fields or by road. If you choose to walk, the right of way is through Manor Farm at Steeple Ashton. Take the road opposite the church gate, and at the end of it turn left. At the end of this road is Manor Farm. You will see Keevil church across the meadows, having passed through the farmyard. The footpath ends at the church. Alternatively, by car continue through the village towards Trowbridge and take the first turn right. After a mile turn right again to Keevil.

The fifteenth century battlemented church at Keevil has a fine nave roof with painted timbers and a churchyard full of interesting carved tombstones. At the end of the road stands Tallboys, a timber-framed house part of which dates back to the late fifteenth century. The village is full of brick and timber-framed houses of great charm. Keevil Manor was built about 1580 with three gabled fronts, and is found in the park near the church. Here lived Anne Beach, who fell in love with the curate, William Winahouse. Her disapproving father locked her in a room over the porch for two years, at the end of which she was given the choice of giving up her lover or losing her fortune. She chose to marry, but died within three months.

Return by car to the crossroads and turn right for **Great Hinton**. In the centre of the village is an attractive pub called The Linnet. From here it is a mile to the A361 Trowbridge-Devizes road. Turn right for **Seend** – a surprising village with some huge, beautiful houses, many of which can be seen from the main road. Much money was made in Seend from the wool trade, and in the fifteenth century a group of Flemish clothiers settled here and left their mark by adding a fine aisle to the church which already existed. It stands on a ridge with a splendid view of the Downs, and is approached between the garden walls of two large houses.

Tour 27: *Villages south of Devizes*

Potterne sits astride the A360 a few miles south of Devizes; it is famous for its church and for Porch House on the main road south of the church. This late fifteenth century timbered building has had many uses through its long history, including that of a brewery, a bakehouse, an inn and even a barracks. It was probably also a church house. It was bought in the last century by Sir George Richmond, who restored it and reconstructed its interior to provide dwellings. It is now a private house with old oak furniture in every room, oak rafters, peepholes and leather thongs lifting the old-fashioned wooden door latches; it can be visited by writing for an appointment (Porch House, Potterne). Two interesting gardens can be visited near Potterne. One is Broadleas (*see* TIC); the other is a small, specialist nursery called The Pygmy Pinetum (*see* TIC).

The other building of immense importance in Potterne is its church. St Mary's is pure Early English, and was built at the same time as Salisbury Cathedral. Potterne was at that time a manor of the

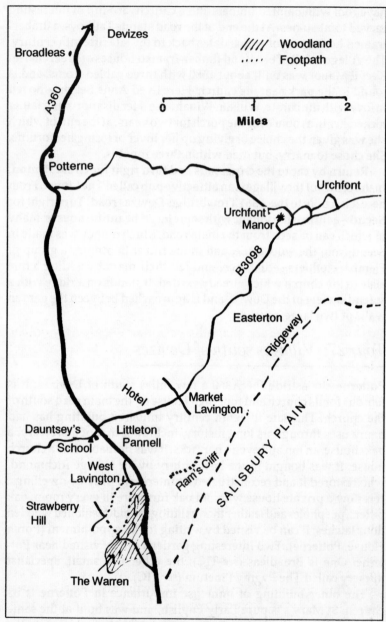

Devizes

Broadleas •

A360

Potterne

Urchfont

Urchfont
Manor

B3098

Easterton

Hotel

Market
Lavington

Ridgeway

Dauntsey's
School

Littleton
Pannell

West
Lavington

Ram's Cliff

SALISBURY PLAIN

Strawberry
Hill

The Warren

//// Woodland
..... Footpath

0   1   2
Miles

Tour 27: Villages south of Devizes

Bishops of Salisbury, and from the late thirteenth century they had a manor house and held the prebend of Potterne, in the chapter of Salisbury. The church is cruciform, with a tower over the crossing, and all windows except those in the tower are lancets, mainly in groups of three. The whole church, except for a small Perpendicular section, is pure, typically unembellished, thirteenth century architecture. The font is exceptional, and is thought to be Saxon. Around it is a text from a Saxon baptismal service, and the translation of the ancient characters is, 'Like as the hart that desireth the waterbrooks, so longeth my heart after thee O

Potterne church interior

God.' Also found in the church is a sculpture in memory of John Spearing – a statue of a woman weeping at an urn. It was carved by E.H.Bailey, who also made Nelson on his column.

Drive south from Potterne to **Littleton Pannell**, a village which merges with West Lavington. Where the A360 crosses the B3098 you will see Dauntsey's School, an old-established private school founded in 1543, which no doubt adds much life to a small village. The old village of **West Lavington** is found further down the Salisbury road on the edge of the Plain, and the more interesting buildings are located near the fine church of All Saints. Take the small road named White Street, and drive to the west side of the church. Near the gate is the Old Manor, wonderfully adorned with thick stems of wisteria and two stone lions on the gateposts.

The church is splendid, with two noble arcades with great circular piers, the Norman north arcade dating from *c*.1200 and the south a little later. The chancel arch was built at the same time as the south arcade, but much is Victorian, particularly the east lancet window. There is an odd small window high up in the east wall, with a figure set in blue stained glass. The Dauntsey Chapel is entered under a wide arch with a pattern of 'D's, and the lifelike reclining effigies of

135

John Danvers and Elizabeth Dauntsey, with books in their hands, seem ready to have a literary discussion. He was a much loved person who died too young, and she a respected lady of 73 at her death.

Ten years ago the Almshouses north-east of the church were dilapidated, but have recently been restored. They were founded at the same time as Dauntsey's School, in 1543, and rebuilt in brick in 1831.

At the end of White Street a narrow track takes the walker up the hill above the village with views across the valley to Rams Cliff and its interesting series of lynchets, with the Ridgeway beyond. Below is the river, its wide pools shining in the woods. The track turns right and soon right again, to descend Strawberry Hill which joins White Street near the church. This half-hour walk affords good views with many church spires to be counted in the valley below.

Return to the crossroads at Dauntsey's School and turn right, taking the road past Clyffe Hotel with its fine Georgian front and equally fine accommodation. Within half-a-mile is **Market Lavington**, a bustling village retaining its market appearance with good shops and services. Here lives Tom Smith. For 200 years, Tom Smiths have been making dew-ponds, a complicated but effective system of producing and retaining water in shallow depressions on top of the bare hills.

Continue to **Easterton**, a village of remarkable timbered buildings, particularly the Manor House at the beginning of the village. Here, as in all the neighbouring villages, the ancient buildings and the population are exposed to the bangs and noises of the army on nearby Salisbury Plain, but it has become an accepted part of life, and military and residents live in reasonable harmony.

On entering **Urchfont** turn left on to the Potterne road. This brings you to the village pond and the church; it is a particularly attractive village. Down the centuries it has had over 60 spellings of its name, many of them found on old maps and documents. In Domesday we find 'Jerchesfonte', and this is thought to mean 'land with a spring on it owned by Jerch or Urch', i.e. Urches Fount. A century ago the village was almost self-supporting, having '3 mills, two forges, one builder, one wheelwright, one tailor, two shoemakers, a saw mill, one saddler, one cooper, one baker, two grocers, one butcher, one taxidermist, two hay tiers, two thatchers, one rat catcher, two carriers, one job master (carriages for hire), a post office, a cheese maker, and, so it is said, seven public houses.' (*Urchfont: a Brief History*, Wiltshire Folk Life Society).

Agriculture on 13 farms was the chief occupation, and so it is today on five farms. It is interesting to note that work on the land did not stop for war. During the last war Land Army girls arrived and worked alongside Italian and German prisoners of war and American troops stationed in Devizes. All worked hard in the fields along with our own troops.

The church of St Michael and All Angels dates from the thirteenth century, although there is evidence of an earlier, possibly Saxon, church. The present building has a chancel arch dating from about 1230, but the greater part of the building is between 1300 and 1500. The chancel, south aisle and transepts all bear witness to the Decorated style, and the chancel in particular with its interior divided into six bays for the remarkable stone vaulted roof. The corbels rest on carved heads, and the carved bosses include St Michael and the Dragon. The carved stem and leaf ornament of the south transept window is of rare beauty, while the porch is about 1430 and in the Perpendicular style.

Urchfont is well known for the residential College of Adult Education at Urchfont Manor. This was built by Sir William Pynsent in the 1670s and the east front was re-designed by William Talman in 1690. In the eighteenth century the house was owned by William Pitt and then by the Dukes of Queensberry. Pioneer work was done in the field of adult education in 1946, when Wiltshire County Council bought the house and grounds and opened it as a residential college providing a high standard of teaching in a wide range of courses. Near the Manor is the Upper Green with more thatched and timbered houses. From here the Potterne road winds through country lanes to rejoin the A360 Devizes road at Potterne.

About the author and illustrator:

Margaret Wilson lives in Murhill near Winsley with her husband and their two boys. They have uninterrupted views of the Limpley Stoke Valley and it was this beautiful Wiltshire valley landscape that inspired her to write about the county and its villages. Her varied career includes working for the British Travel Authority in New York; a complete change of direction found her as a research assistant to her husband first in London, and then in Seattle. Back in England Margaret worked at Dyrham Park for the National Trust.

Margaret and Juliet first worked together on a small book on the architecture of local parish churches. They hope to collaborate on others in the future.

Juliet Greaves presented her first one woman show of landscape paintings in Canada in 1973. This was followed by others in London and Bath. Juliet regularly exhibits her work in the Bath area and has had work included in a winter exhibition at the Royal West of England Academy, Bristol. Many commissioned landscapes, house and animal portraits have been undertaken and her works hang in numerous private collections. The artist lives with her husband and family in Bradford on Avon, Wiltshire.

Urchfont Manor

PROPERTIES OPEN TO THE PUBLIC

Some indication is given in the text but, for precise and up to date information, intending visitors may wish to consult Tourist Information Centres, listed below.

The book, *Historic Houses, Castles and Gardens,* is published annually. It contains details of opening for most properties regularly open and includes those of the National Trust. Available from newsagents and booksellers.

TOURIST INFORMATION CENTRES (TIC)

AMESBURY	Redworth House, Flower Lane Tel: 0980 622833
AVEBURY	The Great Barn Tel: 06723 425
BATH (AVON)	Abbey Churchyard Tel: 0225 462831
BRADFORD ON AVON	The Library, Bridge Street Tel: 02216 5797
CHIPPENHAM	The Neeld Hall, High Street Tel: 0249 657733
CORSHAM	Arnold House, 31 High Street Tel: 0249 714660
DEVIZES	39 St John's Street Tel: 0380 729 408
MALMESBURY	Town Hall, Cross Hayes Tel: 0666 823748
MARLBOROUGH	St Peter's Church, High Street Tel: 0672 513989

MELKSHAM	The Roundhouse, Church Street Tel: 0225 707424
MERE	The Square Tel: 0747 860341
SALISBURY	Fish Row Tel: 0722 334956
SWINDON	32 The Arcade, Brunel Centre Tel: 0793 530328 / 526161
WARMINSTER	Central Car Park Tel: 0985 218548
WESTBURY	The Library, Edward Street Tel: 0373 827158
NATIONAL TRUST	Regional Information Office, The National Trust, Stourton, Warminster Tel: 0985 847777
WILTSHIRE	Press and Public Relations Office, Wiltshire County Council, County Hall, Trowbridge Tel: 0225 863641

WEST COUNTRY Trinity Court, Southernhay East, Exeter, Devon
TOURIST BOARD Tel: 0392 76351

GARDENS OPEN TO THE PUBLIC

Besides the well known gardens open to the public there are many smaller gardens that open either on an irregular basis or on one or two days in the year.

Information on opening as follows: **The National Gardens Scheme (NGS)**, publish annually the yellow book *Gardens Open to the Public in England and Wales*, available from booksellers.

The **Gardeners' Sunday Organisation (GS)** publishes annually the green book *Gardens to Visit* and is sold by booksellers and newsagents.

INDEX of Villages and other places of interest
(indicated in bold type in the text)

More books on a Wiltshire theme from Ex Libris Press are described below:

CURIOUS WILTSHIRE

Mary Delorme

Photography by Duncan Skene

The author digs deeply to tell the story behind some fascinating features of the Wiltshire scene: Water Meadows, White Horses, Sarsen Stones, Dew Ponds, Tithe Barns and Blind Houses.

'A pot-pourri of some of the more interesting features of the Wiltshire landscape. The volume is well produced and contains a number of excellent photographs.'

159 pages; maps and photographs, Price £5.95

THE VALE OF PEWSEY

John Chandler

The Vale of Pewsey, which William Cobbett in 1826 enthused over as 'my land of promise', lies at the geographical centre of the county of Wiltshire. The present author suggests that it also comprises the emotional heart of Wiltshire, 'if by that one means that it embodies the essence of the rural county.' This book is an affectionate but solidly informative account of the Vale of Pewsey, and is the first in our West Country Landscapes series

160 Pages; Numerous photographs and maps; fully indexed; Price £6.95

BRADFORD ON AVON: PAST AND PRESENT

Harold Fassnidge

Photography by Adam Tegetmeier

'... a very successful blend of guide book and history .... Harold Fassnidge has, from his experience in taking visitors round Bradford, become acutely aware of what they wish to know, and presents the salient facts about the history and buildings of the town with skill and charm ... an excellent, well-produced and welcome book.'

136 pages; Numerous photographs; Price £5.95

WHERE WILTSHIRE MEETS SOMERSET

20 Walks in the Country around Bath, Bradford on Avon,
Trowbridge, Westbury, Warminster and Frome

Roger Jones

Illustrations by Edward Dowden

'What a relief the fresh air and sunshine evoked by Roger Jones' walks turned out to be ... all perfectly irresistible.'

118 pages; 21 maps, numerous pencil and pen and ink drawings; Price £4.50

WINIFRED: A WILTSHIRE WORKING GIRL
Sylvia Marlow
Foreword by Pamela Street
Winifred Spencer was born in 1899, the daughter of a cowman and his wife and one of thirteen children. The family lived at Coombe Bake, in the heart of Salisbury Plain. Sylvia Marlow presents the story of Winifred's early life in her subject's own words, a world almost unimaginable today.
123 pages; map and photographs; Price £3.95

CHILD OF THE RED LION
An Hotelier's Story
Molly Maidment
For over seven decades, Molly Maidment has been inseparable from the Red Lion Hotel, Salisbury's old coaching inn, whose origins date back to the thirteenth century. 'It is a beautifully written, warm, evocative memoir ... great naturalness, humour and simplicity.'
135 pages; 18 photographs; Price £4.95

THE SECRET LANE
A Country Story
Ralph Whitlock
Set in the nineteen-thirties, this is the haunting story of an enchanted summer in an English countryside that has vanished forever.
151 pages; double page map; Price £4.95

THE OLD HOUSE AT COATE
Richard Jefferies
Wood engravings by Agnes Miller Parker
'Things have changed drastically at Coate, but the wonderful world that Jefferies loved will always be alive as long as you have this treasure ready to hand.'
175 pages; Numerous wood engravings; Price £2.95

ROUND ABOUT A GREAT ESTATE
Richard Jefferies
Illustrations by Graham Arnold
Introduction by John Fowles
This is a beautiful book: beautifully written and a delight to handle. It could fairly be described as a collector's item.
118 pages; Map and 14 pencil drawings; Price £5.50

Ex Libris Press books are available through your local bookseller or direct from the publisher, post-free, on receipt of net amount; contact —
EX LIBRIS PRESS, 1 The Shambles, Bradford on Avon, Wiltshire, BA 15 1 JS
Phone / Fax 02216 3595
Ask for our free illustrated catalogue